# The Prisoners' M
# Dartmoor ɡ

containing a complete and impartial history of the entire
captivity of the Americans in England, from the
commencement of the last war between the United States and
Great Britain, until all prisoners were released by the treaty of
Ghent. Also a particular detail of all occurrences relative to the
horrid massacre at Dartmoor, on the fatal evening of the 6th of
April, 1815.

C. Andrews

**Alpha Editions**

This edition published in 2024

ISBN 9789362513984

Design and Setting By
**Alpha Editions**
www.alphaedis.com
Email - info@alphaedis.com

# Contents

# PREFACE.

The following pages are presented to the public by one of the survivors of this worst of prisons, believing it will be read with deep interest by every American, and by every relative and friend of those who happened to be one of the unfortunate inmates of the Dartmoor Prison.

If any part of the work should be found languid and tedious, it must be wholly attributed to the suffering situation of the author; the vigor and vivacity of whose mind was greatly affected by those of the body. If misery is less interesting collectively in groups than when viewed individually, let the reader single out one, and view him, separately, through the iron grating, and see him, pale and feeble, etching upon a stick, with a rusty nail, another notch, which adds to his calender another of those dismal days and nights he had spent in confinement; he may view him till he sees the iron enter his soul before he turns from him, and then say—it was my son, my brother, or my friend!—he will then have a picture interesting enough to his feelings.

# CERTIFICATE.

We, the undersigned, late prisoners of war, having been confined the greater part of the last war between the United States of America and Great Britain, and having carefully perused and examined the following Manuscript Journal, kept by Charles Andrews, our fellow-prisoner at Dartmoor, in the County of Devon, in the kingdom of Great Britain, do solemnly declare, that all matter and occurences herein contained, are just and true, to the best of our knowledge and belief; and that this is the only Journal kept at Dartmoor.

| | |
|---|---|
| Capt. Joshua Wait, | New-York. |
| Capt. Samuel H. Ginnodo, | Newport, R. I. |
| Capt. Frederick H. Coffin, | Hudson, N. Y. |
| Mr. Joseph C. Morgan, | Newport, R. I. |
| Lieut. Homer Hull, | —— Conn. |
| Mr. Jacob Evans, | Baltimore, Md. |
| Capt. Benjamin F. Chesebrough, | —— Conn. |
| Mr. Luther S. Dunbar, | Boston, Mass. |
| Capt. Richard Longly, | Portland, D. M. |
| Mr. Ephraim Abbott, | Boston, Mass. |
| Mr. Fenton Conner, | Charleston, S. C. |
| Mr. Joseph Conner, | Newbern, N. C. |
| Mr. David Morrison, | —— Pennsylvania. |
| Mr. Caleb Coffin, | Nantucket, Mass. |
| Mr. John Merrill, | Portland, Maine. |
| Capt. Charles Bennet, | Hudson, N. Y. |
| Mr. William Griffin, | Salem, Mass. |
| Mr. James Bowie, | do.do. |
| Mr. John F. Foster, | Gloucester, Mass. |

| | |
|---|---|
| Mr. Joseph Clark, | Cape-Elizabeth, do. |
| Mr. John Stafford, | Boston, Mass. |
| Mr. Charles Whitewood, | New-York. |
| Mr. Reuben Bunn, | do. |
| Mr. Samuel Rossett, | do. |
| Mr. Jacob F. Taylor, | Philadelphia. |
| Mr. William Conklin, | New-York. |
| Mr. Samuel S. Brush, | do. |
| Capt. John C. Rowles, | Baltimore, Md. |
| Mr. John Meigh, | Boston, Mass. |
| Mr. Edward Shaw, | Baltimore, Md. |
| Lieut. S. S. Fitch, | —— Connecticut. |
| Mr. Samuel Correy, | —— Vermont. |
| Mr. Samuel Howard, | Baltimore, Md. |
| Mr. William Clark, | Boston, Mass. |
| Mr. Joseph Fosdick, | do. |
| Mr. Samuel Morrison, | New-York. |
| Mr. William Hull, | do. |
| Mr. William Atkins, | —— Connecticut. |
| Mr. Daniel Hotchkins, | Salem, Mass. |
| Mr. Thomas Carlton, | Boston, do. |
| Mr. John Migat, | Warren, R. I. |
| Mr. Cornelius Hoy, | Baltimore, Md. |
| Capt. Jesse S. Smith, | Stonington, Conn. |
| Mr. James Sproson, | New-York. |
| Mr. Benjamin Wheeler, | Baltimore, Md. |
| Mr. George Scott, | ——, ——. |

| | |
|---|---|
| Capt. Matthew S. Steel, | Philadelphia, Penn. |
| Mr. W. P. Sevear, | Baltimore, Md. |
| Capt. James McQuilter, | do.do. |
| Mr. John S. Miller, | do.do. |
| Mr. Thomas Bailey, | Salem, Mass. |
| Mr. Warren Humphrey, | —— Connecticut. |
| Mr. William Rea, | Boston, Mass. |
| Capt. Thomas Hussey | Hudson, N. Y. |
| Capt. James Boggs, | Philadelphia, Penn. |
| Capt. James Gays, | —— Virginia. |
| Capt. Thomas Mumford, | Newport, R. I. |
| Mr. Isaac Dowel, | Baltimore, Md. |
| Mr. Frederick G. Low, | Cape-Ann. |
| Mr. Henry Bull, | —— Connecticut. |
| Doct. Benjamin Mercer, | New-York. |
| Mr. Reuben Sherman, | —— Mass. |

N. B.—Out of the above list there are, at this time, only nine survivors, as far as can be ascertained.

# THE PRISONERS' MEMOIRS,
# OR
# DARTMOOR PRISON.

The war between the United States of America and Great Britain, which has been so costly in blood and treasure, and agonized the hearts of so many thousands of our fellow-beings, was formally declared, by a proclamation issued by the President of the United States, in conformity with a solemn act of the supreme legislature of the nation, on the eighteenth day of June, in the year of our Lord one thousand eight hundred and twelve. The nations were, by this act, at open hostilities, and began to capture each other's vessels upon the high seas, wherever found. I myself happened to be so unfortunate as to be among the first captives brought into England. On our first arrival there, we were all collected from different ports, and confined in different prisons. Some were sent to Chatham, some to Hamoze, and others to Portsmouth; where a strict examination took place as to their nativity and citizenship. After the examination, the officers who were entitled to their parole, (such as commanders and first lieutenants of privateers mounting fourteen guns, commanders and first mates of merchantmen, non-combatants, &c.) received it, and were sent to the little village of Ashburton, in Devonshire, or Reading, in Berkshire; the former is situated about twenty-six miles inland from Plymouth, and the principal place of confinement for paroled officers. The town of Ashburton is pleasantly situated in a healthy and fertile part of the country, where every article of provision is more easily obtained and at a much cheaper rate than in many other parts of the kingdom. Here all the officers on parole had their names registered, and particular personal description taken of them. They had allowed them by the British government one shilling and six pence, which is equal to thirty-three and a quarter cents, money of the United States, per day each man. With this small allowance, great numbers of paroled officers were compelled entirely to subsist, for having no other dependence and no friends in this country, they were obliged to purchase clothing, board, and lodging, and all other necessaries of life, and to make use of every economy to prevent themselves from suffering, notwithstanding the cheapness of provisions, and the facility of obtaining them. They were permitted, during the day, to walk one mile on the turnpike road towards London or Plymouth, and at a certain early hour every evening they had to retire to their respective lodgings, and there to remain till next morning; those were their general restrictions for all the days in the week, except two, on which every officer must answer at a particular place appointed by their keepers, in the presence of their agent or inspector. In this manner some hundreds of officers were compelled to drag out a tedious existence in a state of painful solicitude for their country, their homes and families, during the greater part of the late war.

But the condition of the officers on parole was enviable indeed, when compared with that of the officers and others not entitled to that privilege. Every such person taken under the flag of the United States, were sent to some one of the places before mentioned, and confined on board prison ships. The greatest number were sent to the Hector and La Brave, two line of battle ships which were unfit for his majesty's service at sea, and were now used for the confinement of prisoners of war. These were placed under the command of a lieutenant, master's mate, midshipman, and about twenty invalid seamen; there is also a guard under the command of a lieutenant, ensign, and corporal, consisting of thirty-five soldiers to each of these ships.

The Hector and La Brave lie about two miles from Plymouth, well moored by chain moorings. Captain Edward Pelew, of the royal navy, the agent for prisoners of war, resides at this place. On the reception of all prisoners into their respective prison ships, they were obliged to undergo a strict examination concerning their birth, place of residence, and age; a complete and minute description of their person in all respects was taken down in writing. After the examination, there was delivered to each man a very coarse and worthless hammock, with a thin coarse bed-sack, with at most not more than three or four pounds of flops or chopped rags, one thin coarse and sleazy blanket; this furniture of the *bedchamber* was to last for a year and a half before we could draw others. After the distribution of the bedding, we were informed of the rules and restrictions which we must strictly observe. Every ship has a physician attached to it, who is ever to be on board, and when any prisoner is sick, he is to repair immediately to a certain part of the ship for medical aid; but seldom has he any attention paid him till the moment of dissolution, the doctors paying but little attention to the suffering prisoners, although a prisoner is seldom or never suffered to expire on board; for at the moment death seems inevitably approaching, the prisoner is removed to a ship lying near by, called the hospital ship, where if he happen to survive the removal, he receives much better treatment and attendance; but when once removed to that ship, they may bid adieu to their fellow-prisoners, and most of them to sublunary things; for not more than one out of ten ever recovers.

We were then informed, that the Transport Board had most *graciously* and *humanely*, for the health and happiness of the prisoners, imposed on them the following duty; to keep clean the ship's decks and hold; to hoist in water, provisions, coal, and every other article expended or used in the ship;

and also to permit the prisoners to cook their own victuals, which consisted of the following rations allowed by the English government: To each man one pound and a half of very poor coarse bread, half a pound of beef, including the bone, one-third of an ounce of salt, and the same quantity of barley, with one or two turnips, per man. These were the rations for five days in the week; the other two were fish days, the rations for which were one pound of salt fish, the same weight of potatoes, and the usual allowance of bread.

The confinement, and this scanty and meager diet for men who were brought up in a land of liberty, and ever used to feast on the luscious fruits of plenty, soon brought on a pale and sickly countenance, a feeble and dejected spirit, and a lean, half animate body. This bad state of living, I solemnly believe, has been the serious cause of inducing many valuable citizens of the United States to enter the king's service, to the great injury of their country.

The prisoners are counted every night as they are ordered below by the guard; and every morning, about sunrise, each prisoner is obliged to "take up his bed and walk;" for he is ordered to shoulder his hammock and go on deck, and be counted with it on his shoulder. He then leaves his hammock on deck all day, and has permission to go below or remain on deck, as best suits his convenience.

No prisoner is permitted to hold any correspondence, except by unsealed letters passing through the hands of the Board of Transport. No boat is permitted to come alongside the ship, unless by permission of the commanding officer, and then must be strictly examined by the sentry, to prevent any liquor, newspapers, or candles, from coming among the prisoners; these being prohibited by the *gracious* and *humane* Board of Transport.

For consolation in our present miserable condition, we were informed that the said *honorable* Board had indulgently permitted the American prisoners to establish and carry on any branch of manufacture, except such as netting, woollen fabrics, making straw hats and bonnets, &c. &c.; or rather, they prohibited every branch of manufactory which they were capable of pursuing. At this time they could have carried on the making of straw into flats for bonnets with very considerable advantage, as almost every sailor was more or less capable of working at this art, and, by strict attention to the business, could have earned six or eight pence sterling per day: but this was not permitted, and we considered this prohibition a contrivance of the agents of government to induce the prisoners to enter his majesty's service. Their situation was now so abject and wretched, that they were willing to embrace any opportunity where there was the least prospect of bettering their condition, however repugnant to their feelings or sentiments; and though their country's interest was ever nearest to their hearts, yet, through the faint hope of ameliorating their condition, and some day or other of returning to their native land, their wives and families, some of less fortitude were induced to join in arms against their country. It could not be a crime; for self-preservation is the first law of nature.

From the first of our imprisonment, which was shortly after the commencement of the war, prisoners were constantly arriving, and immediately disposed of in one or other of these depots:—among them were great numbers of American seamen who had been delivered up from the different ships of war in the English service, on board of which they had remained from one to ten years, and after receiving many dozen lashes at the gangway of the ships, were sent to prison with the appellation of "dammed rebellious villains, unfit for his majesty's service!"

During the fall of the year one thousand eight hundred and twelve, until April in one thousand eight hundred and thirteen, the English had collected at the following depots the number hereinafter mentioned, who were mostly prisoners delivered up from ships of war, and citizens of the United States detained in them for some time before. At Chatham were collected about nine hundred; at Portsmouth, about one hundred; and at Plymouth, about seven hundred. These unfortunate men had often made application to Mr. Beasley, the agent for American prisoners of war, who resided in England, but were never able to obtain an answer from him. At this time, great numbers of the oldest prisoners were completely destitute of clothing, and the most active and cleanly unable to avoid being covered with vermin.

On the second of April, one thousand eight hundred and thirteen, the Transport Board, apprehending the escape of the prisoners, in consequence of their repeated threats to that purpose, issued an order to Captain Pelew, then agent for the prisoners at Plymouth, to make preparation for removing all the prisoners then confined on board the Hector prison-ship, at Plymouth, to the depot at Dartmoor, in the county of Devon, situated seventeen miles from Plymouth, in the back country.

These orders were accordingly made known to the prisoners; and on the morning of the third of April, they were ordered on deck, with their hammocks, baggage, &c., in readiness to march to a prison, the very name of which made the mind of every prisoner "shrink back with dread, and startle at the thought;" for fame had made them well acquainted with the horrors of that infernal abode, which was by far the most dreadful prison in all England, and in which it was next to impossible for human beings long to survive.

Two hundred and fifty dejected and unhappy sufferers, already too wretched, were called, each of whom received a pair of shoes, and his allowance of bread and salt fish. Orders were then immediately given, for every man to deliver up his bed and hammock, and to repair forthwith into the different launches belonging to the ships of war, which were alongside the ship, ready to receive them. The prisoners entered, surrounded by the guards and seamen belonging to the Hector and La Brave. We were landed at New Passage, near Plymouth, and were placed under the guard of a company of soldiers, equal in number to the prisoners! Orders were then given to march at half-past ten in the morning, with a positive injunction that no prisoner should step out of, or leave the ranks, on pain of instant death. Thus we marched, surrounded by a strong guard, through a heavy rain, and over a bad road, with only our usual and scanty allowance of bread and fish. We were allowed to stop only once during the march of seventeen miles.

We arrived at Dartmoor late in the after part of the day, and found the ground covered with snow. Nothing could form a more dreary prospect than that which now presented itself to our hopeless view. Death itself, with the hopes of an hereafter, seemed less terrible than this gloomy prison.

The prison at Dartmoor is situated on the east side of one of the highest and most barren mountains in England, and is surrounded on all sides, as far as the eye can see, by the gloomy features of a black moor, uncultivated and uninhabited, except by one or two miserable cottages, just discernible in an eastern view, the tenants of which live by cutting turf on the moor, and selling it at the prison. The place is deprived of every thing that is pleasant or agreeable, and is productive of nothing but human woe and misery. Even riches, pleasant friends and liberty could not make it agreeable. It is situated seventeen miles distant from Plymouth, fourteen from the town of Moorton, and seven from the little village of Tavastock.

On entering this depot "of living death," we first passed through the gates, and found ourselves surrounded by two huge circular walls, the outer one of which is a mile in circumference and sixteen feet high; the inner wall is distant from the outer thirty feet, around which is a chain of bells suspended by a wire, so that the least touch sets every bell in motion, and alarms the garrison. On the top of the inner wall is placed a guard at the distance of every twenty feet, which frustrates every attempt at escape, and instantly quells every disorderly motion of the prisoners. Between the two walls and over the intermediate space, are also stationed guards. The soldiers' guard house, the turnkey's office, and many other small buildings, are also within these two circular walls. Likewise several large commodious dwelling-houses, which are occupied by the captain of the prison, doctor, clerks, turnkeys, &c., &c. Inside of the walls are erected large barracks, capacious enough to contain one thousand soldiers, and also a hospital for the reception of the sick. No pains have been spared to render the hospital convenient and comfortable for the sick prisoner. And certainly much credit is due to the director of this humane institution, whoever he may have been, for the attention paid to this most important appendage of an extensive prison. These last mentioned buildings, and several small store-houses, are enclosed by a third wall. These three ranks of walls form in this direction a barrier which is insurmountable.

Thus much for the court-yard of this seminary of misery; we shall next proceed to give a description of the gloomy mansion itself. On entering, we found seven prisons enclosed in the following manner, and situated quite within all the walls before mentioned. Prison No. 1, 2 and 3, are built of hard, rough, unhewn stone, three stories high, one hundred and eighty feet long and forty broad; each of these prisons, on an average, are to contain fifteen hundred prisoners. There is also attached to the yard of these prisons a house of correction, called a cachot; this is built of large stone, arched above and floored with the same. Into this cold, dark, and damp cell, the unhappy prisoner is cast if he offend against the rules of the prison, either willingly or inadvertently, and often on the most frivolous pretence. There he must remain for many days, and often weeks, on two-thirds the usual allowance of food, without a hammock or bed, and nothing but a stone pavement for his chair and bed. These three prisons are situated on the north side of the enclosure, as is also the cachot, and separated from the other prisons by a wall. Next to these is another, No. 4, which is equally as large as any of the others; this is separated from all the others by a wall on each side, and stands in the centre of the circular walls.

Adjoining to this, are situated, in rotation, prisons No. 5, 6, and 7, along the south side of the circular wall. To each prison is attached a small yard, with a constant run of water passing through it.

After viewing this huge pile of building, and obtaining what little information we were able at this time, we were informed that these seven prisons contained a *small family* of French people, consisting of about eight thousand, who were also prisoners of war. Among these fluttering, ghastly skeletons, we were directed to take up our abode, and distribute ourselves as well as we could.

We received our usual hammock and bed, and in conformity with our orders, repaired separately to one or other of six of these prisons; the seventh being allotted to those criminals who had committed misdemeanors, such as murder, larceny on their fellow-prisoners, and other heinous offences, which too frequently occurred.

We entered the prisons; but here the heart of every American was appalled. Amazement struck the unhappy victim; for as he cast his hopeless eyes around the prison, he saw the water constantly dropping from the cold stone walls on every side, which kept the floor (made of stone) constantly wet, and cold as ice.

All the prison floors were either stone or cement, and each story contained but one apartment, and resembled long vacant horse-stables. There were in each story six tiers of joists for the prisoners to fasten their hammocks to. The hammocks have a stick at each end to spread them out, and are hung in the manner of cots, four or five deep, or one above the other. On each side of the prison is left a vacancy for a passage from one end of the prison to the other. We were then informed that the prisoners must be counted out and messed, six together, every morning by the guards and turnkeys.

During the month of April there was scarce a day but more or less rain fell. The weather here is almost constantly wet and foggy, on account of the prison being situated on the top of a mountain, whose elevation is two thousand feet above the level of the sea. This height is equal to the plane on which the clouds generally float in a storm, the atmosphere not being dense enough to support heavy clouds much above that height; almost every one that passes that way finds the top of the mountain enveloped in a thick fog and heavy torrent of rain. In winter the same cause makes as frequent snows as rain in summer. It is also some degrees colder during the whole year than in the adjacent country below. This too is occasioned by the great elevation of the top of the mountain, which is above the atmosphere heated by the reflected rays of the sun upon the common surface of the earth, and being small of itself, reflects but little heat. These two causes combined, produce constant cold and wet weather.

Information was brought us that all prisoners in England were placed on a naval establishment, and under the direction of a naval officer. Captain Isaac Cotgrave, of the royal navy, was the agent for the prisoners of war at this depot. The Transport Board directed that a market should be held every day, in front of each prison yard. This market was supplied with provisions by the inhabitants of the adjacent country; twenty or thirty of whom came every day, and furnished it with every kind of country produce. They were not allowed to impose on the prisoners, by demanding an exhorbitant price for their produce; the prices of every article were fixed by the turnkeys before they entered the yard, according to the prices in the nearest market-town. No person was permitted to enter within the first gate, without being strictly examined as to their business, and without giving a satisfactory account of themselves; if they did this, they were then permitted to enter and begin their trade.

At the market, the French prisoners carry on a great traffic. They buy and sell, and are, apparently, as happy as if they were not imprisoned. But the Americans are not so;—they long for that land of liberty, so dear to them, and sigh for their distant home.

As this depot seems to be the most interesting scene of misery, we shall confine ourselves more particularly to the events which occurred here; only touching, occasionally, upon the most important events of the few prisoners at the other depots.

From the commencement of the war, and previous to April 1813, a great number of prisoners had been sent home, by exchange. Numbers died, and some entered the service of Great Britain. The names of those who died, and those who entered the service, are mentioned in the catalogue hereunto annexed. About the first of May, Captain Cotgrave gave orders to have all the American prisoners collected from the different prisons, and transferred to prison No. 4.

In this prison were about nine hundred of the most abject and outcast wretches that were ever beheld. French prisoners, too wicked and malicious to live with their other unfortunate countrymen: they were literally and emphatically naked; having neither clothing or shoes, and as poor and meager in flesh as the human frame could bear. Their appearance was really shocking to human feeling. The mind cannot figure to itself any thing in the shape of men, which so much resembled the fabled ghosts of Pluto, as these naked and starved French prisoners. Much of the misery and wretchedness of these creatures was owing to their imprudence and bad conduct.

These men were now to be our associates, and we deprived of the privileges allowed heretofore to prisoners of war. As the gate of this yard is always kept shut, we could have no advantage of the markets, or connexion with the other prisoners; while the French prisoners, in the other prisons, were allowed those benefits.

The American prisoners now began to experience a new scene of distress;—the little clothing they had when they were taken, was either worn out or disposed of at a very reduced price, (not more than one tenth of the value,) to buy the very necessary articles of soap and tobacco.

We remained in this situation during the month of May, one thousand eight hundred and thirteen, close confined in prison No. 4, with the liberty of that one yard. We often demanded of Captain Cotgrave, the reason why such distinction was made between the American and French prisoners; but were never able to obtain any other reason, than that his orders were issued from the Transport Board to do so. This month we received letters from our fellow-prisoners at Chatham, and those on board the prison ships at Plymouth; who informed us of every particular of their situation at both places; but they were comparatively well off, when compared with our situation. The prisoners at Plymouth informed us, that other prisoners arrived there daily, and that they expected shortly to be removed, and to participate with us in the sufferings and misery of Dartmoor.

On the twenty-ninth of May, the garrison which we found here, was removed and supplied by new regiments of soldiers. We learned, that no regiment is stationed here more than two or three months at a time. These guards consist of about twelve or fifteen hundred soldiers, who have been guilty of some offence, disobedience of orders, or neglect of duty; and are sent here as a punishment. By these soldiers we were informed of the particulars of the actions of the Java and Peacock.

At this time we made known, in as respectful a manner as we could, all the particulars of our unhappy situation to Mr. Reuben G. Beasley, agent for American prisoners of war. We informed him that our allowance was too scanty, that the whole day's allowance was scarcely enough for one meal, that the greater part of the prisoners were in a state of nakedness; and also, that great numbers had enlisted out of the prison, into the king's service;— that they had been compelled to do it, in hopes to better their condition, and indeed to preserve life. For, as they were wholly neglected by the agent of their country, they saw no other means by which it was possible to preserve existence—or ever to return to their country; as they totally despaired of any exchange.

At the same time we informed him, that unless something was done soon for our relief, we must all either (though reluctantly) enter the service of the enemy, or fall a sacrifice to famine and want.

We informed him also of the distinction which was made between the French and American prisoners. The former were allowed many privileges and advantages, which were denied the latter; and that our treatment was contrary to what we considered the custom and usage of civilized nations in modern warfare. That we were hurried into the prison-house before dark, locked up, to remain without any light or fire till seven or eight o'clock in the morning.

If a prisoner had to leave his hammock, *per necessitatem*, he was obliged to grope from one end of the room to the other, and often could not regain it during the whole night.

To all these petitions, complaints, and remonstrances, Mr. Beasley returned no answer, nor took any notice of them whatever; which, of course, made every prisoner despair of any relief from him. These letters could not miscarry, or be intercepted; for we had formed a course of correspondence with several very respectable mercantile houses in London, through which our letters were sure to reach Mr. Beasley by private conveyance.

The month of June commenced with deep distress; for disease was then added to nakedness and famine; and we were still more severely dealt by. For Doctor Dyer, who was head surgeon of the Hospital-department, would not permit an American prisoner to be brought into the hospital, until his complaint was completely confirmed, and often not until he was so weak, and reduced so low, that it would take four men to remove him on his hammock. For this conduct, he justified himself by saying, that he had been acquainted with the impositions of the Americans during the revolutionary war, and that these impositions were not to be played off on him any more.

A moment's reflection must have convinced him, that it was impossible for these men not to be sick, in their starved, naked and wretched condition; sleeping in a prison, whose walls were constantly wet and cold, occasioned by the constant rainy, foggy, and damp weather on this mountain.

But he refused to admit the American prisoners into the hospital, because, he said, such numbers would breed every kind of pestilence and disease among the French prisoners. We attributed these evils to the shameful and criminal neglect of the agent of American prisoners, whose conduct deserves the severest censure of every prisoner, and requires a strict and impartial investigation by the authority of his country.

From the first to the fifteenth of May, we were every day called out of the prison and counted, to see if any remained in prison. The soldiers then entered the prison, and searched every hammock; if they found any prisoner, he was hastened out into the yard, though they were often found so weak and feeble, that it required assistance to enable them to walk.

The guards discharged this duty with great reluctance; their feelings often revolted, when compelled to do this unkind office, and though accustomed to scenes of distress, were very sensibly touched at the miserable situation of these their fellow beings.

On the eighteenth of May, we received letters from the other depots, and were informed that there were seven hundred prisoners at Plymouth, on board the Hector, which was so much crowded, that Captain Pelew, of the Royal Navy, and principal agent of the Board, had received orders from the Board, to remove the prisoners to other depots, either to that of Chatham, Dartmoor, or Stapleton, which is near Bristol. This last place was fixed on by the Board as a necessary precaution to prevent any disturbance, which was apprehended might arise, should too many American prisoners be confined in one place.

Accordingly, on the twenty-eighth, Captain Pelew ordered two hundred and fifty to be landed from the Hector and marched to Dartmoor. They arrived there on the same day, and after going through the same manœuvre as the first draft, they were committed to No. 4. These, together with the former draft, made four hundred and seventy Americans, and seven hundred naked outcast French, all intermixed in one prison.

Care was taken to keep the yard of this prison always locked, to prevent us from going to market. By this means, all we obtained from the market came through the hands of the French prisoners in the other prisons, who obliged us to pay twenty-five per cent. above the market price for all we had. At this time, about thirty were missing out of the number, some dead, and others had enlisted into the king's service.

On the twenty-ninth, fifty more American prisoners were transported from on board the Hector, in a ship of war, round to Chatham. Two only at a time were permitted to come on deck; the others were compelled to remain below, without hammock, bed, or blanket. I leave the reader to judge whether this measure arose from wanton cruelty in those immediately concerned, or whether it was absolutely necessary to prevent their escape, or rising and taking the ship, which had her whole crew on board.

On the thirtieth, two hundred prisoners were ordered to go ashore, who accordingly made themselves ready, and landed at New Passage, under a guard of seamen and marines. Here they were received by a guard of soldiers, consisting of two hundred and fifty, who were to convey them on foot one hundred and thirty-four miles to Stapleton, within a few miles of Bristol.

Stapleton is a pleasant situation, and is a fine healthy country; but the fatigue of the journey, the restrictions and inconvenience to which the prisoners were subjected, presented to them a melancholy prospect.

At the commencement of their journey, they were provided with a shilling (twenty-two and a half cents) per day, for their traveling expenses. This was all the allowance made them to purchase food, drink, and lodging; and they were to perform the whole journey in eight days. They were also particularly enjoined not to leave the ranks on pain of death, and the guard had orders to despatch any prisoner who should attempt to escape. The particulars of their march, their arrival at Stapleton, and treatment at that place, will be mentioned hereafter.

On the first of July, two hundred more were ordered from on board the Hector, to march and share with us the miseries of Dartmoor. They were landed as usual, and marched under a strong guard to that mountain of wretchedness, and after passing through the usual forms at their arrival, were received into prison No. 4, and might justly have exclaimed, in the language of an eminent poet, "Hail, horrors! hail, thou profoundest hell! receive thy new possessor." For every one ordered to this prison, counted himself lost.

On the third of July, another draft of prisoners, consisting of about two hundred and fifty, were taken from the Hector, and sent to Stapleton, under the usual guard, allowance, and restrictions.

The fourth of July, the birth-day of our nation, had now arrived. The American prisoners, feeling that fire of patriotism, and that just pride and honor, which fills the bosom of every American, when that great day of jubilee arrives, roused all their drooping spirits, and prepared to celebrate it in a manner becoming their situation. We had by some means obtained two American standards; and being upward of six hundred in number, we divided into two columns, and displayed our flags at each end of the prison. Of the propriety of the proceedings, I leave the reader to judge. We were, however, resolved to defend them till the last moment: but Captain Cotgrave, either from a determination to depress our spirits as much as possible, that we might the more readily be induced to enter the service of the king, or that an enemy's flag should not be hoisted in their country, ordered the turnkeys to enter the prison-yard, and take the colors from us. We returned him an answer, that the day was the birth-day of freedom, and the anniversary of our nation; and that he would confer on us a particular favor, if he would permit us to enjoy it with a decorum and propriety suited to our situation as prisoners of war. We added this *arrogant* condition, that if he should persist in attempting to take that flag which we should ever respect, in whatever country we were, he must abide by the consequences. Captain Cotgrave, being irritated at this haughty and independent language, ordered the guard into the prison-yard to take the standards from us. An obstinate resistance was made. After some time spent in fighting for the flags, the guard obtained one: the prisoners bore off the other in triumph, and secured it. The remainder of the day was spent in harmony and quietness. At evening, when the guards came as usual to turn us into the prison, a dispute arose upon the pitiful revenge sought for in depriving the prisoners of their flag. This soon grew into an affray; the guards fired upon the prisoners, and wounded two, which ended the affray.

From the disturbance on the evening of the fourth, nothing remarkable took place, the prisoners being generally tolerable quiet and peaceable till the tenth, when a dispute arose between the French and American prisoners in the yard of No. 4; the dispute was quite warm, and pervaded nearly all the prisoners of both nations, each of whom espoused the cause of his fellow-prisoner. Things were not pushed to extremities this evening, the hour to turn in prevented their further progress; but animosities had not subsided. At this time the French prisoners occupied the two upper stories of prison No. 4; they consisted of about nine hundred outcasts from the other prisons, as we had occasion to mention before. They had during the night, with malice prepense, concerted a plan to massacre the Americans. With this design, they had provided themselves with knives, clubs, stones, staves, and every kind of weapon they could obtain.

Thus armed, they had managed to be in the yard first in the morning, and arrayed themselves to give battle as soon as a sufficient number of Americans should come out. Accordingly, when about one hundred and twenty had entered the yard, this group of naked malignity began the attack with desperate fierceness; the Americans, unsuspicious of an attack, were of course unarmed, and at first could make no resistance; but after recovering from the surprise which so sudden an attack had created, they made an attempt to rally; but the Frenchmen cutting off their retreat into the prison and preventing those within from joining or rendering any assistance, soon caused the Americans to fall a prey to their superior number. Before the guards could interfere to prevent the further proceedings, the Americans were mostly stabbed or knocked down with heavy stones, and mangled in a most shocking manner. What would have been the issue, had not the guards entered, and by charging on both parties put a stop to the battle, is difficult to tell. On examining the wounded, (fortunately none were killed,) it appeared that about twenty on both sides were badly, and many others slightly wounded. The former were taken to the hospital, and though apparently dangerous, in a short time all recovered. Captain Cotgrave immediately informed the Board of Transport of this unhappy event; but painted it in such dark colors on the side of the Americans, that the Board gave answer, that the Americans were totally different from all other men, and unfit to live in any society. "If the household be devils, what is the master of the house?" Did not the Americans descend from England?

The yard of No. 4 was ordered to be divided, which was done by a wall fifteen feet high, which cut off all communication with the Americans, and their late meager associates. This act, though it seemed to have been done to injure the Americans, certainly created no regret; for instead of doing them an injury, it was a great relief to be disencumbered of that outcast tribe.

A spark of momentary joy may burst through the darkest clouds of grief, and hope for a moment make us forget our miseries. On the twenty-ninth of this month, Captain Cotgrave received orders to remove one hundred and twenty Americans from this prison to Chatham, which was to be the complement of a cartel ship then lying at that place; this embraced the greater part of the prisoners captured before January, 1813. There remained of those captured before and after that time, 1200 at Chatham, 400 at Stapleton, and a few less than 500 at Dartmoor, some on board the prison ships, and a number of officers on parole at Ashburton. The greater part of these had been delivered up from ships of war.

At the close of this month, forty-five were found to have entered the service of the enemy, and fifteen had died at this place, seven or eight at Chatham, and not one at Stapleton.

At the commencement of August, we found ourselves limited and very much straitened in our regulations. We were not permitted to go out of the yard. A more alarming scene of distress than any we had before experienced, now presented itself before us, and death seemed to be the inevitable lot of every man.

The King of Terrors daily reached forth his inexorable hand, and removed the sufferer from the pale of this clay tenement; for the small-pox had got among the prisoners, and its ravages were so alarming, that every prisoner expected each day would be his last; for numbers died daily.

The prisoners who remained able, collected themselves together, and formed a committee of correspondence, who, by bribing the guards, conveyed letters daily to Mr. Beasley; particularly describing their situation, that they were almost naked, and defrauded by the Contractor of half their rations, which before were but one-third enough. That the small-pox had got among them, and numbers died daily—that they were covered with *animalcula*, and unless he could do something for their relief, they must all perish together.

To these complaints he paid no kind of attention, neither came to see whether they were true or false, nor sent any answer either written or verbal.

The reader can easily figure to himself what must have been our feelings, when five hundred men, closely confined in one apartment, with that mortal epidemic among them without any assistance, or possibility of escape.

The evil must lie somewhere; we were in doubt whether to believe it was the will of the general government, of the people at large of this country, or whether it was not entirely the fault of our agent, in not seeing that all the officers in whose immediate care we were, acted the honest part in the performance of those duties, which both this government and that of the United States had intrusted to them. It was not a general thing, and the evil was near at hand. The prisoners at Halifax fared well; they did not, nor could not, complain; prisoners in other places in England were tolerably well provided for.

After so many fruitless applications to our agent, we despaired of any relief from that quarter, and then made application to Captain Cotgrave, and demanded of him, what provisions the government of England made for prisoners of war, when neglected by their own government. He gave us every opportunity to search out the fault, by producing the following printed rules and regulations, made by the Transport Board.

The honorable Transport Board have made arrangements with certain agents or contractors, to supply all prisoners of war, as follows:

Each prisoner to receive per day, for five days in the week, one and a half pounds of coarse brown bread; one-half pound of beef, including the bone; one-third of an ounce of barley; the same quantity of salt; one-third of an ounce of onions; and one pound of turnips. The residue of the week, the usual allowance of bread; one pound of pickled fish, and just a sufficient quantity of coals to cook the same. These to be served out daily by the contractors.

We watched the contractor, and found he weighed all the articles at once, neat weight; and saw him scrimp the weight, to fill his pocket out of the prisoners' bellies.

On beef days, the whole is thrown into a large copper; when it is sufficiently boiled, the bone is taken out, and each mess, consisting of six, receives twenty-seven ounces of beef, and one gallon and one pint of soup.

On the fish days, every mess boiled their potatoes and fish in a net made of rope-yarn, that they might have it separately to themselves; after it was boiled, it was taken up in wooden buckets, with which each mess were provided; and each prisoner, being also furnished with a wooden spoon, sets round the bucket, on the wet floor, and makes a fierce attack.

After making these, and some other demands, which we considered ourselves entitled to, most of which were immediately granted, but some delayed, as we shall note hereafter, our sufferings were somewhat relieved.

Could not these have been removed by our agent long before? We find but few men so honest that they do not need looking to sometimes by those who are interested in their honesty. These contractors would have been as honest as many other men, with sharp looking after. Was it not, then, the duty of Mr. Beasley to see that the prisoners had what the government of England allowed them? If it was not, what was his duty? Was he sent there, as the log of wood in the fable was sent by Jupiter into the pond, to be god for the frogs?

We found, by the printed regulations delivered us by Capt. Cotgrave, the government allowed each prisoner a hammock, one blanket, one horse-rug, and a bed, containing four pounds of flocks; these articles too were to serve us two years. By the same regulations, the prisoners were to receive for clothing, every eighteen months, one yellow round-about jacket, one pair of pantaloons, and a waistcoat of the same materials, as the government of England allow for their soldiers; and one pair of shoes and one shirt, every nine months. The shirt, though coarse, was a change which we had not had for a long time before. All these we demanded and received; we also received a woollen cap, which was to serve us eighteen months.

I cannot leave this subject without some little description of several of the articles of clothing. I will begin with the cap, and take them in their natural order, from head to foot.

The cap was woollen, about an inch thick, and seemed to have been spun in a rope-walk, but much coarser than common rope-yarn. The jacket was not large enough to meet around the smallest of us, although reduced to mere skeletons by such continued fasting; the sleeves came about half way down the arm, and the hand stuck out like a spade; the waistcoat was short—it would not meet before, nor down to the pantaloons—thus leaving a space between of three or four inches; the pantaloons, which were as tight as our skin itself, came down to the middle of the shin. The shoes, which was the pedestal for all the ornaments above, were made of list, interwoven and fastened to pieces of wood an inch and a half thick. The figure we made in this dress was no common one.

"*Spectatum admissi risum teneatis amici?*"—HOR. A. P.

"My friends, were you admitted to see this sight, could you keep from laughing?" When you see us tackled, and put upon runners—skeletons as we were.

By the regulations handed us, we also found that the Board allowed a sweeper to every hundred men, to sweep and keep clean the prison, who was to be taken from among the prisoners, and allowed by the government three pence per day; and one out of every two hundred was allowed four pence halfpenny a day for cooking. In like manner, a barber had three pence; and the nurses in the hospital, six pence a day. All these offices were occupied by Frenchmen, as was also the employments in the mechanic arts at six pence per day.

During this month great numbers died of the small-pox, and some of other diseases. Several entered the king's service. Suspicions had arisen, that several taken in arms against Great Britain, were British subjects; they were consequently taken out, and charged with having committed high treason. That they were taken in arms against Great Britain, was not denied; but that they were her subjects, which was the most essential part of the charge, could not be proved; they were consequently acquitted, and remanded to prison.

We had but one clear day during the whole month of August.

September commenced, and we remained in the situation just described. The prisoners continued very sickly.

Men, otherwise commonly honest, when reduced to extreme necessity, naturally resort to the commission of crimes. It is a maxim strikingly true, that "hunger will break through a stone wall;" and it is equally true, that it will break through all moral obligation. Honesty and integrity are but mere chimeras in dire necessity. Such was our situation, that it resembled more a state of nature than a civilized society. Petty larcenies were daily committed among the prisoners; brothers and the most intimate friends stealing from each other. To provide a remedy against this evil, we appointed a legislative body, to form a code of laws for the punishment of all such misdemeanors. A tribunal was also formed to try and convict all criminals according to law and evidence. Many were tried, found guilty, and sentenced to receive twenty-four lashes equally as severe as is given at the gangway of a man-of-war ship.

To show the force of habit, though it is a vicious one, we will give the reader a striking example. Some of the prisoners were so attached to chewing tobacco, that they sold all their day's allowance of beef to the French at the gate, to purchase one chew. They sometimes sold this allowance to buy soap enough to wash one shirt, but this was only enduring one evil to remedy a worse.

By letters received from our fellow-prisoners on board the Crowned Prince, and the Nassau, prison ships at Chatham, we received information that the Americans were distributed among the French prisoners on board the several different ships at that place, and very severely used; that they had vainly addressed Mr. Beasley, and that several had died and numbers entered the British service.

By letters received from Stapleton, we were informed of the particulars of their march from Plymouth, which we promised to give the reader in a former part of this work. The reader will remember, that at the commencement of their journey, they were allowed a shilling a day for traveling expenses, and on their way, they had to pay three pence a night to lodge in a barn, or some public building, on straw. As they were allowed a shilling only, this took one-quarter of the whole. With much ado they reached Stapleton; they found the prison at that place well constructed for the convenience of the prisoners, within a short distance of the city of Bristol; which is the third city in England, and situated in Somersetshire, at the conflux of the river Avon, with the small stream of the Froom, about ten miles from the mouth of the Severn; these, and several other small tributary streams, running through a fertile country, bring into market all kinds of provisions and fruits common to the country, which are sold at a much cheaper rate than at most other places in the kingdom. From these sources, the market at Stapleton, which is kept every day at the prison, is supplied with all kinds of market produce. On their arrival they found five thousand French prisoners. There are three prisons enclosed and garrisoned in the same manner as those at Dartmoor; they were distributed among the French prisoners in the different prisons. They had also written to Mr. Beasley several times, and informed him, that their situation was bad, although much better than that at Dartmoor, and required his attention. But he was determined to take no notice. They therefore concluded, that no arrangement was to be made for their exchange, or that any assistance was to be offered from the government of the United States, made necessity an excuse for entering the service of the enemy of their country; which many did at that place.

How far this is a crime, when we consider the *quo animo*? I shall take this opportunity to show what is the custom of nations, and what appears to be the law of nature. It is said, "If a person be under circumstances of actual force and constraint, through a well-grounded apprehension of injury to his life or person, this fear, or compulsion, will excuse his even joining with either rebels or enemies in the kingdom, provided he leaves them whenever he hath a safe opportunity."

Now to return to Dartmoor. At a time when the prisoners had despaired of any relief, and began to reconcile themselves to their hard fate, they were very agreeably surprised to hear that Mr. Reuben G. Beasley had condescended to visit them, and then waited at the gate for admittance. The idea, that their deliverer had come, diffused a general joy through the whole prison, and "lighted up a smile in the aspect of woe." The soldiers and guards were ordered into the prison, and turned out every man, both sick and well; overhauled the hammocks, swept the prison, and opened the window-shutters: all filth was removed and every thing made clean, for the first time since our arrival. The guards were then stationed at the door, to prevent any prisoner from going in, to have any communication with the agent: we were told, that no man could speak to him, or have any communication with him whatever. At three o'clock, the entrance of Mr. Beasley was announced by the turnkeys. We arranged ourselves in the yard, in anxious expectation of the glad tidings he might bring. He appeared, attended with his clerks, the clerks of the prison, and a very numerous train of soldiers. As he entered the yard of the prison, we presented a frightful appearance, in our yellow uniform, wooden shod, and meager, lantern-jaws. He felt the sight, and seemed much surprised at the group. We stood in silent expectation; he moved along to the prison; but how were our feelings damped at this moment! when we expected from him the language of consolation and relief, he only uttered, in a careless tone to his clerks, "that he did not think that the number had been so great!"

He entered, and cast his eyes around the cold wet walls of the prison, and seemed to say, with a shrug of his shoulders, "I am glad that it is not I that is to live here." When he returned, we were determined to have some conversation with him. We therefore collected round him, demanded what arrangements were made for our relief, whether we must expect to remain in our present condition? Telling him, that if we must, that we could not long survive; and presenting him with a list of names of those who had already entered the king's service; and telling him all the particulars of our distress. He then opened his mouth, and said, he had no power to do any thing, nor any funds to do with; but he would do his endeavor. We asked him the cause of so great a difference in the treatment of the prisoners here and at Halifax? There they had all the necessaries and conveniences of life; here we had none of them. We asked him to whom we should apply for relief in future? We told him we had been to great expense, heretofore, and much trouble, in conveying letters to him, while he had not thought fit to answer. He said the exchange of prisoners was stopped for the present year, and that we could not expect to have our condition altered. With these unwelcome observations, he went immediately out of the gates, and left us to all the wretchedness of despair.

We returned into the prison, lamenting our fate. Some cursed the day they were born; some, the day of their captivity; some attributed all their sufferings to the inattention of the Agent, and others, to the government of the United States. We retired to our hammocks, and gave vent to our feelings in sighs and tears.

The thought that we must forego all the endearments of life, and perish together, in a foreign country, among our enemies, was too much for our feelings to bear. The groans of the disconsolate and sick filled the whole prison. Our Agent not empowered to act, and without funds! We had now only to look to heaven, whose will it was to bring us to this state, and through whose mercy alone we could hope to find relief.

The winter was fast approaching, and the cold upon this mountain was very severe. The small-pox still continued, and the measles had got among us, and great numbers were sick with both diseases. The next day, conceiving they had no other alternative, a great number entered the British service; rather hazarding the chance of escape, and censure of their country, than to trust life to the perils of this prison.

Although I am a little before some part of my story, I must not forget to mention, that about the middle of September, another draft was taken from the Hector, now at Hamoaze, near Plymouth; among which were the crew of the United States' brig Argus, taken by the Pelican. One Robinson, who had belonged to the Argus, had declared, that several of the crew of that vessel were British subjects. And immediately seventeen, whom he pointed out, were taken and conveyed on board the receiving ship, St. Salvador, and put into close confinement, there to await their trial and execution, should they be found guilty. The boatswain, and a number of others, wounded in the action, were conveyed to the hospital, in Mill-prison at Plymouth.

At the end of this month a great number had died, and numbers down with all complaints, prevalent in crowded camps or prisons. The weather much like the month before.

By letters, received the tenth of October, from Chatham and Stapleton, we were informed, that Mr. Beasley had visited them, and his conduct and language at those places were the same as at this depot. By the letters from Chatham, we had an account of eighteen making their escape, by cutting a hole through the side of the Crown Prince, at that place; that afterwards the guard were increased and more vigilant.

On the sixteenth, Capt. Cotgrave gave orders, by directions of the Transport Board, to have all these outcast Frenchmen in No. 4 collected. This took four hundred and thirty-six from the prison, and much relieved us.

Before I proceed with the remainder of my story, I cannot but here observe the strange effect habit and corruption have in changing our common nature. They had been many of them ten years in this prison in a state of perfect nudity, and had been so for many years; had slept upon the bare stone-floor without covering for many years, till the flesh had acquired a sort of hardness, like the stones themselves.

This was the effect of gambling, which had acquired a greater power over them than hunger or nakedness. Whenever they were supplied with clothing, they never put them on, but turned to gambling, till they had lost the whole. They had often been supplied by their countrymen in the other prisons, with hammocks, beds, and clothing: but they no sooner got possession of them, than they went to the grating of the other prisons, and sold them, and gambled the whole away. It is difficult for the mind to conceive, how human beings could be possessed of fewer virtues or more vices; or how they could any further change their common nature to a bestial one without the assistance of a Supreme Being. It is a remarkable fact, that these men (if they yet deserve the name) were more healthy, though stark naked winter and summer for ten years, than any prisoners at this depot; though to the number of nine thousand.

The French prisoners never received any assistance from the French government, but depended entirely on the British. Though I cannot praise the general acts of the latter government, nor am I disposed to flatter; yet they did a humane act which certainly deserves credit. They took these four hundred and thirty-six Frenchmen out of this prison, clothed them well, and put them on board a prison-ship at Plymouth, separate from all other men, except their guards, who carefully watched them, and prevented them from disposing of their clothes, and kept them decent during the remainder of their captivity.

In the six prisons, occupied by the French prisoners, is carried on almost every branch of the mechanic arts. They resemble little towns, being mostly soldiers; every man has his separate occupation; his work-shop, his store-house, his coffee-house, his eating-house, &c., &c.; he is employed in some business or other.

There are many gentlemen of large fortunes here, who having broke their parole, were committed to close confinement. These were able to support themselves in a genteel manner; though they were prisoners, they drew upon their bankers in other parts of Europe.

They manufactured shoes, hats, hair and bone-work. They likewise, at one time, carried on a very lucrative branch of manufactory. They forged notes on the Bank of England, to the amount of one hundred and fifty thousand pounds sterling; and made so perfect an imitation, that the cashier could not discover the forgery; and very much doubted the possibility of such imitation.

They also carried on the coining of silver, to a very considerable advantage; they had men constantly employed outside of the yard, to collect all the Spanish dollars they could, and bring into prison. Out of every dollar they made eight smooth English shillings; equally as heavy, and passed as well as any in the kingdom.

Whether they are constituted by nature to endure hardships, or so long confinement has got them wonted to live in prisons, I will not venture to say; but they really seem easy under it, live well, and make money to lay up.

They drink, sing and dance, talk of their women in the day-time, and, like Horace, dream of them at night; but I have not heard of any issue by this visionary connexion. But the Americans have not that careless volatility, like the cockle in the fable, to sing and dance when their house is on fire over them.

When any one has committed a crime, or becomes a nuisance among them, he is condemned, and sent to No. 4, to remain during his captivity; so the Americans must dwell among the damned.

On the twenty-eighth, a large corps of French prisoners, taken at the battle near St. Sebastian, in Spain, arrived at this depot, and took their abode among the other Frenchmen. At this time, a very mortal distemper prevailed among the French prisoners, that carried off eight or ten every day.

When any one dies in the hospital, his body is removed to the dead-house, a place made for that purpose; after being stripped of his clothes, shirt and all, (which go to the government, or the nurse of the deceased,) the body is then opened, to learn the nature of the disease; it is afterwards, quite naked, put into a coarse shell, made of rough pine boards, and remains in the dead-house for several days, till a number is collected in the same manner: when a sufficient number is heaped together to call their attention, a large hole is dug back of the prison, and all thrown in together, without form or ceremony.

The hospital department consists of a surgeon, two assistants, and as many male nurses as are necessary. Every morning, at nine o'clock, orders are given, by the ringing of bells, that every prisoner, wanting relief or medical aid, must repair to the hospital to be examined, and receive prescriptions; he then returns to the prison, where he remains till carried in again.

The sickness among the Americans somewhat abated the latter end of this month. Many entered the king's service. As the recruiting officers receive a premium on every soldier they enlist for his majesty, they used every inducement in their power. An officer belonging to a Dutch regiment, thought it a good opportunity to *mock de gildt*, entered the yard, and began to solicit men to enlist into the regiments to go against the United States; but the Americans took this the greatest insult, that such a booby should think of getting *them* to fight against their country; they soon hustled Mynheer out of the yard, and frustrated all his hopes of gain.

The majority of the prisoners used every means in their power to prevent our countrymen from entering the enemy's service. We often, on discovering the intention of any one to enlist into their service, fastened him up to the grating and flogged him severely, and threatened to despatch them secretly if they did not desist; but attempts were vain; they justified themselves on the plea of self-preservation; that there was a possibility of escaping and saving their lives; and if detected by their country, their death was distant, but here it was speedy and certain.

Capt. Cotgrave, perceiving the great exertions that were made to prevent any entering his majesty's service, adopted a plan to encourage it. When any one was known to be disposed that way, he would send him a line, and invite him to come to the guard-house, where the other prisoners could have no communication with him: here he was kept till a number sufficient for a draft was collected, then sent to Plymouth, and put on board a receiving ship, and received their bounty. About one draft a month commonly took place.

*November.*—The weather is much similar to that of the State of New York at the same season; rain, snow, and hail, almost every day; the prisoners without stockings, and many had been so unthoughtful of the future as to sell their jackets to buy food; and the whole dress allowed them was no more than sufficient in the most clement season, the prisons being always damp, and the weather very rainy. We were allowed no fuel; some had also sold their hammocks, blankets, and beds, to the French. These thoughtless wretches were now obliged to sleep, or rather lie, upon the stones the whole night, and when there happened a fine day, which was seldom, it was with the greatest difficulty the guards could rouse them from this stupor, and get them into the yard. We dreaded the winter.

We received letters from our fellow-prisoners at other prisons, informing us that they had applied to Mr. Beasley, and advising us to do the same, which we had already done; they wished to be informed of our situation; this was done in poetry.

The time had now expired for relieving the present guard; this being done, its place was supplied by a Scotch regiment. Sympathy glowed in the minds of these gallant fellows; no nobler act has nature done than form the heart that feels for others' woes. They felt for ours, and though enemies, at the peril of life relieved them; it was an act that superior beings might behold with admiration. Touched with this tie of nature, when ordered to bring out every prisoner into the yard, sick or naked, they often pitied him, gave him some relief, and left him behind; though ordered to cut him down or run him through, if he offered to remain.

They supplied us with late papers, and gave us all the account they could of the affairs in America. They cheered us with the agreeable account of the Essex, and her success in the South Seas: we had friends that pitied us, though they could not greatly relieve us.

About this time a few prisoners from Plymouth, lately captured, and lately from the States, arrived at this depot.

The news they bring of the success of the American arms, animates every soul, and for a moment we forgot our troubles. By them the account of the Boxer and Enterprise, the complete victory of Commodore Perry on Lake Erie is given us, but no hope of exchange or prospect of peace. No alteration in our treatment by government; the prisoners not permitted out of yard No. 4. The French go any where through the several prisons; go to market, but the Americans not permitted to. The government grew more strict in their enlistments; they would receive none but regularly bred sailors, and no invalids.

At the latter end of this month a great number of prisoners, taken under the American flag, claimed a release from confinement, and showed that they owed their allegiance by birth to powers in alliance with Great Britain. To Holland, Sweden, and other places, and are released on account of their neutrality.

Weather very cold all the month. The prisoners without shoes or clothes, obliged to keep their hammock. Fewer deaths than the month before. Yard covered with snow.

*December.*—Cold increasing. Prisoners in despair. Capt. Cotgrave ordered the prisoners to turn out every morning at the hour of nine, and stand in the yard till the guards counted them; this generally took more than an hour. Many of the prisoners were without stockings, and some without shoes, and many without jackets. They cut up their blankets to wrap up their feet and legs, that they might be able to endure the cold and snow while they were going through this ceremony. We complained to the captain of this practice, and told him it was too severe for the prisoners to endure; he said it was his orders, and as agent he must obey them. We reminded him of several instances that must shock the heart of every feeling man, that he himself was knowing to the day before. Several of these naked men, chilled, and benumbed with cold, and being half starved, fell down lifeless in his presence, and in presence of the guards and turnkeys. This was a cruelty which exceeded murder in any shape whatever; to expose the naked helpless prisoner to perish in the pitiless blast of this bleak mountain, was an act that made our hearts recoil with horror.

We remonstrated with the infamous author, but all our supplications and remonstrances were in vain; the wretch was inexorable; his feelings had become callous by continuing so long among the sufferings of the French prisoners. After these men fell down in the yard, they were taken up and carried to the hospital, and with some difficulty were restored to life again; they were then immediately sent back to prison, there to lie on the stone floor without bed or covering.

At this treatment I presume the reader will not so much wonder that so many died, as he will that any could live at all.

The name of Isaac Cotgrave, agent at Dartmoor, of cruel memory, will ever be engraven, in odious characters, on the mind of every American who witnessed his unparalleled cruelty.

On the 22d of this month the iron sceptre was wrested from his hand, and placed beyond his reach. A new agent, Capt. Thos. G. Shortland, at this time superseded Cotgrave. Shortland was a man whose feelings had not yet grown callous by being familiarized with human misery, and at his first arrival he was shocked at the scenes of our misery, which presented themselves in every shape before him; touched with compassion, he could not continue the cruel practice of counting over the prisoners every morning in the yard. He countermanded the order which his predecessor pretended to have been commanded to put in force. He declared to us that he would do all in his power to procure us some relief from his government; that he himself would do all he could in his situation as agent, to assist us; he very politely and kindly offered to forward to Mr. Beasley, or to the Congress of the United States, any communication or petition which might procure us any relief. He stated in feeling terms to the Board of Transport the real condition of the American prisoners. He ordered the doctors' assistants to visit the persons daily, and to remove to the hospital all the sick who had before been refused admittance. He granted permission for two of the prisoners to attend the market each day, and purchase such little necessary articles as they were able, such as soap, potatoes, tobacco, &c.

These relaxations in the morning of his power seemed to promise a bright day; but the noon began to grow a little obscure, and, we are sorry to say, at last went down in blood, and left obscure the bright traits of the morning.

The weather was incredibly cold upon this mountain; the moor, as far as the eye could extend, was covered with frost and snow; the prison walls, by being continually damp, had become like solid ice, and the prisoners obliged to keep their hammocks, for being allowed no fire, had no other means to keep themselves warm.

The rigor of treatment seemed somewhat relaxed; for our friendly officers and Scotch guards gave us as much relief and consolation as their station would permit, and we endeavored to cultivate their friendship.

According to Capt. Shortland's advice, and our own necessities, we again made application to Mr. Beasley. In this letter we informed him that we were fully of opinion that the United States would sanction any reasonable overtures he should make to prevent her citizens from starving or perishing for want in a foreign prison; that his being agent for the United States was sufficient power, and he had a right to pledge the credit of the United States, which was amply sufficient to procure any sum requisite for our relief. We farther stated, in the most unequivocal terms, that unless some relief was given us soon, that the prisoners had come to a unanimous and final determination to offer our services *en masse* to the British government, and at the same time transmit to the United States a copy of all letters from us to him, and set forth to Congress all our reasons for so doing, which would most undoubtedly cast all the blame on him.

This month ended with increased cold, and snow falling daily. The prisoners did not go out of their hammocks, only at dinner, which was the only meal they had.

*January, 1814.*—The year commences with as cold weather as we ever experienced in the city of New York; the buckets in the prison, in the short space of four hours, froze ten or twelve quarts to a solid, and the prisoners must inevitably have frozen, were not the hammocks placed so near together as to communicate the animal heat from one man to another.

The running stream that supplied the prison froze solid, and the weather was allowed to be colder than it had been for fifty years before.

On the 1st the snow was two feet on the level, and began to snow again; the cold somewhat abated, and it continued snowing the greater part of the time till the nineteenth; it had now got to be four feet on the level, and the drifts in the yards as high as the prison walls (fifteen feet), the water all frozen, and the prisoners obliged to eat snow for drink. The guards were all obliged to leave the walls and retire to the guard-house; no sentry on duty except in the barracks.

At midnight; this dreary night, eight prisoners, thinking to take advantage of the night to make their escape, as no sentries were in sight, formed a ladder, and with it ascended and descended the first wall directly against the guard-house, and in ascending the second, the soldiers in the guard-house discovered them, and apprehended seven; the eighth got quite over the wall, and made his escape. These seven were taken to the guard-house and there put into the black-hole, which is the place for prisoners that attempt to make their escape: the weather extremely cold, was likely to prove their last. But the fifth day they were removed to the cachot, and remained on two-thirds allowance, sleeping on straw for ten days. The prisoners, soldiers, and officers, were now furnished with salt provisions, which are always kept at the prison against any emergency of this kind. Every man upon the mountain was now much alarmed, as only ten days' stock of provision was in reserve on the mountain, and there were now upwards of nine thousand French and American prisoners, besides fifteen hundred soldiers and officers, doctors, and a numerous train of turnkeys.

## LINES,

## BY AN AMERICAN PRISONER.

On the 14th day of January,
This night ordained by Fate,
For eight poor Yankee sailors
To try for their escape.

Seven of them detected were,
And in the guard-house lay;
The eighth resolved on liberty,
By chance he got away.

The night, being dark and dreary,
And he had far to go,
So this poor Yankee sailor
Got hobbled in the snow.

Discovered by his enemies,
That forced him back again,
Within the walls of Dartmoor,
Oppressed with cold and pain.

Shortland, bred a seaman,
In Neptune's school was taught;
His heart compressed with pity,
Methinks I read his thought—

Saying, go into the guard-house,
And set those eight men free,
I'll show the sons of liberty
There's honor still in me.

The back house was at some distance, and the snow drifted in from ten to fifteen feet deep; this formed an impassable barrier; but Capt. Shortland, at the head of two hundred French prisoners, all the horse of the garrison, and clerks, turnkeys, &c., after working one whole day, shovelled a passage sufficient for wagons to pass. For should the weather continue as cold as it then was, all communication between that place and Plymouth, whence the provisions were brought, being totally stopped by the great depth of snow, they were in danger of starving. On the twenty-fifth the weather began to moderate and the snow began to dissolve.

The eighth man, who made his escape, had wandered over the moor, through the deep snow, till by chance he came to a single hut on the moor; the peasants suspected him to be a prisoner, as no person could travel in such tedious weather, and after examining him some time, he confessed he had made his escape from prison. They brought him back, and he received the same sentence as his unsuccessful companions. During his absence, all the officers and prisoners were much concerned at the miserable fate they were confident he must have shared, as it was impossible for him long to live, for if he survived the storm, he must starve in a few days: but it seemed he had reached the hut on the second day, without being frozen in any part. The officers and guards considering his attempt so bold and fearless of death, and showed such a noble longing for liberty, were really sorry to see him brought back, and declared that a man so dauntless as to dare such perils, deserved his liberty, and a reward; and had it been in their power he would have been released.

Here I must beg leave, though I fear the repetition of our distress may tire the reader, to appeal to the feeling of my fellow-citizens, at this time at ease beyond the great Atlantic: what would you have done, could you have seen your fellow-citizens at Dartmoor, the coldest winter there has been for half a century, without fire or light, during the night, without stockings, and many without shoes, and nearly naked, half starved, buried in snow, upon the top of an uninhabited and uncultivated mountain, the camp distemper among them, and overrun with vermin; great numbers dying, and death grimly threatening every man?

Say, would you not have pitied and flew to their relief, and left the gay circle of your amusement?

But few entered the service of the enemy this month; the weather being so very cold, they dreaded the removal to Plymouth.

*February, 1814.*—The weather was more moderate, and snow dissolving very fast.

We received a letter from Mr. Beasley, for the first time since our confinement, which had continued ever since April, 1813. This is the first scrap in writing any prisoner in England had ever received from him. It reads as follows:—"Fellow-citizens, I am authorized by the government of the United States to allow you one penny halfpenny per day, for the purpose of procuring you tobacco and soap, which will commence being paid from the first day of January, and I earnestly hope it will tend towards a great relief in your present circumstances. I likewise would advise you to appoint a committee, by which means you can convey to me any intelligence through the Board of Transport." Immediately after the reception of this letter, we formed a committee of six, five besides myself, who were to see that every man had his money, and gave a receipt to Capt. Shortland, who was authorized by Mr. Beasley to pay it.

In conformity to these arrangements, we received, on the 5th of February, three halfpence sterling per day (less than three cents). This money was to be paid every thirty-two days: as one month had passed from the time it was to commence, we received the payment for all that time. The day's allowance of cash would purchase two pounds of potatoes, or three chews of tobacco, which latter was five shillings and six-pence sterling all over England. We returned to Mr. Beasley a letter, acknowledging the receipt of the money, and stated the great alteration this little attention had made in the prisoners; every man was animated beyond description to find himself again acknowledged by the United States; that before that time they concluded that during the twelve months they had been immured in prisons, so far from their country, that they were entirely forgotten by her, and that she did not any more remember she had such sons as those at Dartmoor. The gloom that had so long clouded their countenances now began a little to disappear, and the prospect a little brightened, and we had hopes of life; but still our nakedness was grievous to bear. In a letter of thanks to our government, through the medium of Mr. Beasley, we stated every particular of our situation, our past and our present sufferings. We stated to him that it could not be possible that the Congress of the United States had allowed that small sum for those few articles, and had not made any provision for clothing, which ought to have occupied their first attention, for without clothes we did not need soap. We must, therefore, conclude this sum was allowed by himself out of the United States funds, and that we were extremely grateful for it; that the United States, were they acquainted with all the particulars of our situation, would make immediately all requisite arrangements for clothing, which his Honor Mr. Beasley must be well satisfied we were much in need of. After this correspondence with Mr. Beasley, we formed resolutions to expel all gambling, and were fully confident that some greater arrangement would be made for us.

Before this time seventy-five had entered the British service out of nine hundred Americans at this depot; but now not a man mentioned such a thing; he could not be persuaded to do it. This shows how much effect so little attention of Mr. Beasley had upon the prisoners. We, on the 22d of this month, petitioned to have the black prisoners separated from the white, for it was impossible to prevent these fellows from stealing, although they were seized up and flogged almost every day. Our petition was granted, and we greatly relieved, and the blacks, ninety in number, occupied the upper stories.

The weather greatly moderated, but vast quantities of rain fell. The British government made an order to release all prisoners belonging to the King of Prussia, taken under the flag of the United States. A few days after they issued a general order, that all prisoners belonging to any nation with whom she was in alliance, under whatever flag they were taken, should be released. This order released many Americans, who were acquainted with different languages, and could make a plausible story: the Yankees were citizens of all nations whose language they knew.

At the close of this month, we received letters from our countrymen on board the prison-ships at Chatham, and likewise those at Stapleton, informing us that they had received the same allowance of three halfpence per day at both places, at the same time that we received it. They also sent a copy of a letter of Mr. Beasley, which is the same as the one already mentioned. They also mentioned that they had had a very severe winter, but it was not as severe there as at this place. The prisoners at Chatham, among whom were great numbers that had been released from the British service during the winter, had received their wages and prize money; which, as is usual with a generous-hearted sailor, they distributed for the good of the whole. At the depot at Stapleton, the American prisoners were distributed among the French, who, in many instances, were very kind.

On the last day of this month, by papers conveyed to us by our friendly Scotch guards, we found an account of Captain Porter's taking two large South-Seamen, mounting 16 guns, and upwards of fifty men each. He says they surrendered without firing a gun; that they were taken by the boats of the Essex, and speaks rather slightly of the courage of the British on those occasions.

In March the weather began to be mild; the snow was now mostly gone; the prisoners could remain in the yard the greater part of the day, and their spirits were much revived at the expectation of receiving their penny halfpenny per day in a lump; but this was prolonged, and the prisoners began to despond, as they had received no information from Mr. Beasley since the second of last month; but on the fifteenth orders were issued to pay it, and glad enough were we, for every man considered this little payment his sole support.

The gates were now left open, and we had all the privileges of the market which were allowed the French; we were allowed to go through all the prisons, visit the French officers, and gain all the information we could from London papers, which many of the French officers took daily. The French prisoners were much concerned at the fate of their country when they learned the success of the allies, as every prisoner had been in the army or navy of Bonaparte, and were much attached to the Emperor.

Having received no letters from Mr. Beasley, we now gave up all hope of exchange, gave ourselves up to our condition, and resigned our destiny into the hands of Heaven to deal with us as he pleased, during the long captivity which we believed we had to endure; for, seeing the English papers filled with accounts of the success of their arms in Europe, and every day declaring their full confidence of a complete conquest of America, we could not expect peace, though this boasting did not frighten us, for we knew the strength and valor of the American people.

On the 18th we established a coffee-house in our prison, as the French had in theirs, and sold coffee at a penny a pint; but you cannot think it very delicious when I inform you that it could not be bought under two and three pence per pound, and molasses seventy per hundred weight. At the same time some of the prisoners received money from home, and all established themselves in some kind of business. Some established themselves as tobacconists; others as potato merchants, butter merchants, and indeed almost all kinds of merchandise were carried on in our prison after we received our second payment: we had "free trade and sailors' rights." We could purchase any article of provision in the markets; coffee, sugar, molasses, any thing the country afforded. The gates being now opened, we traded with the French. We could buy potatoes at six-pence a score, butter at one and six-pence per pound; and as for meat, that was out of the question altogether. Every man began to use all the economy he could, which he perceived the French did. Some went to work for the French at making straw flats, at which they could earn one penny per day. Others were employed in making list shoes, some in the manufactory of hair bracelets, necklaces, &c.; while great numbers employed themselves in working the bones we got out of the beef, in imitation of the French, who were very ingenious, and would form the most admirable and beautiful ships, plank, mast, and rig them all of bone. The French, for their amusement, had regular plays in a theatrical form, with very elegant scenery, once a month. Hamlet's ghost was an easy part to act, for they had only to show their natural visage, being mere shadows themselves. They had excellent music, and appropriate comic and tragic dresses. They also had schools for teaching the arts and sciences, dancing, fencing, and music, and each of these in great perfection. As numbers of them were daily receiving money from France, their prison was very rich. But No. 4, where the sons of liberty had lived so long on the vapor of a dungeon, when will the same be said of you? Perhaps some victim as unhappy as myself, when some ten years have rolled away, and the human mind, compelled by stern necessity to invent, and I myself have found my *quietus* behind the prison-walls, may tell a sorry story of splendid misery within your gloomy gates.

During the whole month of March the weather was quite mild, and the prisoners gained their health and strength greatly. On the 21st we detected the contractor cheating us in our rations, by giving scant weight. We immediately informed Capt. Shortland of the fraud, who examined into the fact, and had the cheating stopped, but gave the conduct of the contractor a very easy term, by saying it was a mistake.

Towards the close of this month many of the Americans had obtained some remnants of garments from the French, and mostly all the boys had got into the employ of the French officers as waiters. Many of these little victims of war were under thirteen—and there were many old men above the age of sixty imprisoned: both these classes it has been considered contrary to the custom of nations to imprison. What use could it be to sacrifice the aged or the child in a prison?

I had sailed for many years in the employment of merchants of England, and had ever had a most exalted idea of the humanity and generosity of that nation, but by woeful experience I found I had been deceived. Many of my readers may, perhaps, dispute the truth of what I have here asserted; but I appeal to thousands of my countrymen, who will testify the truth of what I have said, and thousands who have suffered with me will say, that the pen of Homer or Milton would fall short in describing the miseries of Dartmoor.

Though the weather was quite mild at the end of the month, yet, as many of the prisoners were almost naked, they suffered greatly for want of more clothing.

On the last day of this month we received a letter from Mr. Beasley, being the second ever received at this depot from him.

I shall commence the transactions of April by giving a copy of the letter which we received the day before.

*Fellow-Citizens,—*

In addition to the allowance of three halfpence per day, which has heretofore been allowed, I shall make remittance to Captain Shortland, to enable you to have coffee and sugar twice a week, that is, the days on which your rations consist of fish; my intention at first was to have the articles themselves sent to be distributed, but it being suggested to me by the committees at the other depots that the value in money would be more serviceable to the prisoners, I have determined to allow three-pence halfpenny per man, two days in the week, being the value of those articles, and I hope the committee will find means to ensure its being applied to the purpose intended.

Yours, &c.,

R. G. BEASLEY.

With the letter was accompanied an additional allowance, which augmented the sum to two pence halfpenny, and we now received the sum of six and eight pence on the eighth. This was to continue being paid monthly.

As it is natural to expect, this payment produced great spirits and animation among the prisoners, and was as welcome as a thousand pounds when we were free and had plenty. With this money the prisoners purchased many little necessary articles of clothing, such as shirts, shoes, trowsers, &c., which could be bought very cheap of the French, who always kept stores of second-hand clothing, which were obtained from the officers.

The weather was fine—for this place—and the prisoners healthy; and, having obtained some clothes, and anticipating the reception of more, began to be quite comfortable in their situation, when we compare it to the distress of that cold winter they had just passed through.

Our little salary seemed to command some respect from the turnkeys, soldier-officers, and subalterns, who were themselves as poor and meager as Romeo's apothecary. It brought us many indulgences, such as full liberty of the markets, which before had been prohibited, and we compelled to purchase of the French at the gratings. This was a great benefit to us, for we could now trade with the country people much cheaper.

To regulate our rations, we were also allowed to appoint a committee of two, to attend at the store-house to see that the contractor gave us weight in those articles allowed by the Board.

The day after we received our payment, we received London papers containing an official account of the allies entering Paris, and the complete defeat and downfall of Bonaparte. This news was a sore affliction to the French prisoners, who were passionately attached to the Emperor, and not much less galling to the Americans; for now some boasting pettimaitres among the British officers would come into the yard, in the most taunting, vile manner, to sport with the feelings of the prisoners of both nations:

"For," said they, "we have conquered France, and have not the least doubt but we shall shortly completely reduce the United States to colonies of Great Britain, and your haughty President become a mendicant vagabond." This insolence was too much for flesh and blood to bear. They declared they could have peace on any terms they wished, and, although we were yet prisoners of war, they considered us their subjects.

Such language to prisoners who could not resent it, showed that the authors of it could be nothing better than the vilest caitiffs, and could flow from nothing but the meanest of envy.

The French prisoners felt this conduct much more severe than we; for the conquest was already made, and they were obliged to look to a master whom they hated, to one who was the choice of their enemies, Louis XVIII.

Many gentlemen visited the prison to congratulate those unfortunate men on their being restored to liberty, and thought that as they had been many of them confined from five to eleven years, they would rejoice at the idea of liberty under any monarch. They presented the prisoners with the old national flag, and advised them to wear the white cockade; but they declared, in the presence of those gentlemen, that they would prefer staying in prison all their lifetime than to serve any other master, or become subject to any other king than Bonaparte, whom they loved. But the sequel will show how lasting their determinations were, and how like they were to their nation at large.

At this time to express their regret at the misfortune of their beloved emperor, and their resentment to the proffered flag and cockade of the new monarch, they came forward every man, wearing the tri-colored cockade, and the white ones on the heads of the dogs that ran about the yards. The white flag they destroyed with great eagerness, in presence of the visitors and great numbers of British officers standing on the wall.

Shortly after this intelligence of the affairs of France, we had letters from Chatham, which informed us that, since the last from that place, there had arrived great numbers of prisoners there, and that many were almost persuaded in their own minds to enter the enemy's service; that they had received the additional allowance at the same time as ourselves. On the 15th we were informed that there was a draft ready at Plymouth, and would shortly be sent to this depot.

About this time a separate arrangement was made for allowing the crew of the U. S. brig Argus half pay, to be received monthly, and at the time the first payment was received, they received clothing. This was an additional benefit to our prison, as there were established in it a great number of shops for various branches of business; this money circulated within ourselves, and every one derived some advantage.

The preliminaries of peace being agreed on at Paris, the French prisoners, towards the close of the month, began to make all preparation for leaving the prison, and once more visiting their native country. The idea of returning to their native land, their homes, and their wives, was too nicely interwoven with the threads of their nature to be razed by that of their aversion to the Bourbons. The change which was about to take place in their situation had in it too many of the endearments of life to be sacrificed for the love of any monarch. The scenes of their youth, the places where they had spent so many careless, pleasant days, the embraces of their friends, all rushed upon their minds at once, and they could not forbear the highest transports of joy. They went to leave all the evils that men suffer in this life, and to embrace all the good and blessings of it.

We had now an opportunity of procuring all the tools and utensils of the mechanical arts which the French carried on. And during their long imprisonment they had obtained almost every article that could be named; all these articles we purchased, and every man turned all his ingenuity to some branch or other.

The weather being pleasant, and the prisoners healthy, they bore their confinement with as much patience as could be expected. By permission, towards the close of the month, they established a beer-house, where small-beer was sold for two pence halfpenny per pot.

On the last day of the month a school was established for the instruction of the boys in the arts of reading, writing, and common arithmetic; to maintain the school, the rate of tuition was fixed at six pence per month per scholar, to be paid by them.

May commenced, the weather was equally fine, but some rain. In the bustle of the crowd, we almost forgot our situation; the market square was crowded every day with people of every description—some came for curiosity, others to trade, and among the latter were many Jews, who brought clothing, and many other articles which might be wanted by the French for their journey. The French prisoners were all in confusion making ready for their departure. The proposal was again made to the French prisoners to hoist the white flag, and wear the insignia of Louis XVIII.; but they rejected it, and would not listen to any argument. Now was the time to try the strength of their attachment to the emperor, whom only they had sworn to serve or die in prison. When the proposition was made to them either to hoist the flag and wear the insignia, or remain in prison till the last draft of prisoners in England, they then immediately, but rather reluctantly, hoisted the white flag and put on the cockade. But it was a grievous sight to them, and they could not look at it but with the bitterest reflection, and the most poignant regret; for they had for years endured all the calamities and hardships of danger and war for the support of their beloved emperor, who now must give place to those they hated.

On the 10th a draft of Americans from Plymouth, about 170, in great distress, arrived at this depot, among whom were the seventeen that were taken and put into close confinement by the information of Robertson. They had been tried for high treason by a court of judicature, but there not being sufficient evidence on the part of the crown to support the charge, they were acquitted, and sent to this prison, to be dealt by as prisoners of war only. In the same draft were a number of prisoners who had been released from British ships of war.

On the 15th we received our monthly pay; this came very appropos, to enable us to buy all the furniture used by the French at a very low price. On the same day Mr. Williams, clerk to Mr. Beasley, and a Jew merchant of London, Mr. Jacobs, brought and delivered to each prisoner a jacket, pair of trowsers, a pair of shoes, and a shirt. The jacket and trowsers were of very coarse blue cloth, much coarser than that of the English; but it was such a dress as we had been used to wearing. Mr. Williams then told us that we were to be clothed altogether by the United States, and these we had now received were to last us eighteen months. These were the first we had ever received from the agent; and it is impossible to describe the great change and life it gave the prisoners: they all cleaned themselves, and every thing about them, and laid by their yellow rags.

They began to attract the attention of all about them; the British officers would now visit them, and were not afraid of being covered with vermin as before; our appearance was not loathsome to one another; we were in great spirits now, and to prevent some thoughtless men from selling their clothing to the French to wear home, we passed an act that every man should appear in his dress which he had received from the United States, to receive his monthly payment, or not receive it at all.

We now felt a spirit of independence which had before been smothered in the wretchedness of our situation; we could now converse with ease, and without that restraint which a mean and dirty habit will ever give a man in presence of those in a clean and genteel one; that old, dirty, tawny dress depressed us with a sense of inferiority; but now we could vindicate our country's rights in argument with any visitor; we came out boldly, and demanded restitution for any injury or fraud that heretofore had been practised upon us; every man began to see to it, how he should gain something more, now he was furnished with utensils, and set himself about something.

On the twentieth, orders arrived for the first draft of French, and the day after five hundred were taken out and marched to Plymouth, where they took shipping and went to France.

A very singular kind of conduct now showed itself in the British government. Twenty-four Americans, citizens of the United States, who had been taken under the flag of France about two years before the war between the United States and Great Britain, were now among the French prisoners at this place. They had often applied to the government to be released as citizens of the United States before the war. They also, asserting their citizenship, had applied after the war, to be enrolled on the list of United States prisoners, but had been refused both their applications. They now expected to be released with the French prisoners, on account of their always being considered by government as French prisoners; but the government would not release them as such, but detained them in prison. They now, seeing they could not have the privilege of French prisoners, applied to Mr. Beasley, and claimed their citizenship in the United States, but received for answer from him, "that he could not receive them as such!"

These men were citizens of the world sure enough, for they belonged to no nation in it; they therefore remained unprovided for by either government. But we could not see them perish as long as we had any thing which could be divided; they therefore lived upon our charity the whole time.

On the twenty-fifth, another draft took place as before, and released one thousand. At this time, all the Swedish subjects, taken under the flag of the United States, were released and permitted to go home.

The French, who had been employed in different occupations, being now released, we applied to government to be allowed that privilege, each man employed at these different occupations, such as carpenters, blacksmiths, masons, nurses in the hospital &c.; and two hundred labourers were paid six pence a day. In answer to this application, we were told, that after the discharge of all the French prisoners we should have them allowed us.

When the French prisoners passed out, they were all called over by name, and great numbers being dead, which was not known to the keepers, afforded a fine opportunity for the Americans to answer, and pass out in the name of the deceased. Great numbers, who could speak French, obtained their release in this manner.

At the end of the month, another draft of one thousand took place, among whom, twenty Americans passed out in the same manner as before, the deception not being as yet discovered.

At the same time, we received information by letters from Chatham and Stapleton, that Mr. Williams, and the Jew merchant had visited them, and supplied them in the manner as ourselves, and also, that the French prisoners at those places were released daily. Few died this month, the weather generally pleasant, but much rain.

Before I leave the events of this month, I cannot forbear mentioning one very melancholy and striking instance of the force of disappointment and despair; where hope has painted glowing scenes of pleasure; the heart sickens and the mind grows frantic.

On the discharge of the prisoners, every man before he can be discharged, must return the same complement of bedding which he had received two years before; he must have the same number of articles, let them be in ever so worn-out state; if he do this he can then pass, if not, he cannot pass.

It happened, that one unfortunate man, called for in the last draft, did not bring forward the articles of bedding: he was refused a pass, and ordered back to produce them; he ran about in great confusion and the most terrible anxiety to procure them, but could not find them; he returned again to pass out, he was refused; he had been immured and buried within the cold, gloomy walls of this prison, eleven tedious and painful years, he said: he ran and looked, and looked again—he could not procure them, and he was refused to pass;—then, in the agonies of despair, he seized a knife and put an end to his sufferings, by cutting his own throat, in presence of his countrymen and the keepers!

The spectacle was too horrible to behold without the deepest regret and sorrow; it was a sight, that all-powerful Juno might have sent down *Iris* from heaven, to relieve his struggling soul from her united limbs. Many, through despair, had committed suicide before in the French prisons.

June. The weather continued much the same. On the fifth, another draft of French prisoners was made. At this time, an order was issued, to discharge from confinement all French prisoners who had been taken under the flag of the United States. The Americans, who were ever watchful for an opportunity to make their escape, took advantage of this order to obtain their liberty; many came forward and claimed their birth right in France and its dependencies; being well versed in the French language, they bore a good examination, and one hundred and twenty-one were released in the last draft of French subjects.

By this time all the French from No. 4 were released, and we had the whole prison to ourselves; but the blacks being mixed with us were very troublesome.

We having purchased from the French all they had, were now well furnished with household furniture, such as tables, dishes, seats, and things to cook in. We now carried on the business of making straw flats for hats and bonnets, although not allowed by government; by strict attention, we could make at this business three pence a day.

On the fifteenth, we received our monthly pay, which never failed to come about that time.

On the twentieth, the whole of the French prisoners were discharged except a few sick in the Hospital.

On the 22d, Capt. Shortland gave us information that all the prisoners in England were to be collected at Stapleton, as the Transport Board determined on that place for a general depot for all American prisoners. There were now in England, three thousand five hundred unparoled prisoners. The same information was given at Chatham and Plymouth.

We anticipated much advantage in the change of situation, and began to prepare for the removal, and from the authentic account we had received from that place, there had not died but one-fiftieth as many in proportion to their number, as had died at this depot; the change was therefore much to be desired; the climate was much more pleasant and healthy, and the contiguity to the city of Bristol, where every article manufactured by the prisoners, would find a ready market at a much higher price than at this place; all articles of provision much cheaper. But much to our disappointment, on the twenty-fourth, the late order was countermanded, and Capt. Shortland ordered to make all things ready for the reception of all the prisoners in England, as the board had determined on making this depot the general receptacle for all prisoners in the country, as they considered it the safest of any in the kingdom, and they might have added, far more infernal than the Bastile. He also told the prisoners that he had orders to employ any number of the prisoners he should think necessary, such as carpenters and masons, to build a church near the prison, and a number of laborers to repair the roads; also blacksmiths, coopers, painters, lamp-lighters, and nurses in the hospital, &c. The number, he said, would amount to upwards of one hundred. He then told us under what restrictions we were to work; we were to be under the eye of a guard all the time, and if any prisoner attempted to make his escape, that no more Americans would be employed, and to prevent this, the following rule was adopted; they were to receive their pay, at the rate of six-pence per day, every three months, and if any prisoner escaped, the whole pay was forfeited; this kept every prisoner watchful over each other, for when one run away, all the others lost their whole pay and employment; besides, this was the method they had used with the French.

We found this to be a great benefit to us, for those workmen who went out of the prison yards, smuggled in all kinds of prohibited articles, such as rum, candles, oil, and news papers; and smuggled out all the prohibited articles, manufactured in the prison. At this trade each man could make four or five shillings a day.

There were now eleven hundred prisoners, and manufactures having got to considerable perfection, the receipts of money brought into the prison each week besides the allowances, were fifty pounds sterling. Besides this sum of money, many prisoners had friends in England, and received from them considerable sums.

The prisoners now began to live, and got into good spirits. The latter part of this month 150 workmen were employed at different branches of mechanical business. At this time prisoners from Stapleton arrived at this depot; their number at first was 400, but was now reduced to 350. Seventeen had enlisted in the British service, eight died, and the remainder made their escape. On their arrival here, they were committed to No. 4, which contained upwards of 1400, and was much crowded. These 350 were in a very bad condition, many were without shoes, and had travelled most of the distance in the same condition, for the shoes they had received from the agent did not last more than three or four weeks. This was an imposition of the contractor, as the agent afterwards said he had learned.

On the twentieth of June we were informed, by Capt. Shortland, that when the other prisoners arrived from Chatham, he would open the yards on the south side of the enclosure, and give us all the privileges of the other prisons. These yards being large, would admit of many amusements which that of No. 4 would not, such as playing ball, &c.

At this time, viewing our circumstances on all sides, and seeing no hope of exchange or peace, we formed a design to make our escape; our plan was, that immediately after our removal to the other prisons, to dig a hole two hundred and eighty feet long, all the way under ground; this would reach from the prison beyond the outer wall. The success of this design will be mentioned hereafter. On the same day we received London papers, containing an account of the capture of the United States frigate Essex, by the frigate Phebe and sloop-of-war Cherub. The London editor said that the Essex was equal in size to a seventy-four. Had he said her defence was equal to a seventy-four, Capt. Hillyar would have agreed with him. The garrison was again renewed with a new regiment, and the old one removed. This regiment was very much embittered against the government; their term of five years, for which they had enlisted, having expired, the government refused to discharge them.

At this time the government was giving great encouragement to soldiers to enlist to fight against the United States; this regiment was offered every inducement to join; they therefore made it their business to make particular inquiry of the prisoners what was the manner of our warfare, and the dispositions of the American soldiers. I found they were very ignorant in these things, and easily deterred from their enlisting. I composed a song, and distributed it among them, after which not a man ever enlisted or offered to. This very much enraged the soldier-officers of the garrison, who issued orders that if any sentry was found conversing with a prisoner, he should be punished; but it was impossible to stop it, the soldiers were equally desirous as the prisoners to converse.

The fourth of July was not far distant, and we began to make preparations to celebrate the day a second time since our confinement. We obtained permission from the keeper to purchase two hogsheads of porter; we likewise had got a number of gallons of rum unbeknown to the keeper.

We also provided ourselves with American colors, and invited all the soldier-officers, clerks of the prison, and soldiers, to attend and hear an oration that would be delivered on the fourth, which was the anniversary of American Independence. The prisoners were in high spirits, expecting to enjoy themselves much better than they had done on the preceding one, when they were half naked.

In the month of June we had but few deaths, and the prisoners generally healthy; we had rain, and many showers.

On the first of July we received letters from Chatham, informing us that they were much concerned at a late order, which was shortly to remove them to this depot; the same letter informed us that the prisoners on board the Crowned Prince had been confined three days without victuals or drink; the reason why is yet untold.

On the second of the month the crew of the Argus received another payment of several pounds each man, through the hands of the late purser to that vessel; this came very timely to us in the celebration of American Independence.

By letters from Plymouth, this day, we were informed the reason of the prisoners being confined below deck on board the Crowned Prince.

It happened that the boats' crew of that ship had been on shore and stole a sheep from a farmer, and the commander had had his table served with the best pieces; the farmer getting information where the sheep had gone, came and demanded reparation for his sheep; the commander, to screen the boats' crew, paid the farmer the price of the sheep.

The story of the sheep was soon known to the prisoners, who, having a dislike to the commander, one morning, as he was going on shore with his wife, and at the moment he was entering the boat, they all as one agreed to cry *blar*; he understood the meaning the very instant the sound struck his ear, and turning back, he ordered the prisoners all below, and to be kept there three days without victuals or drink.

On the evening of the third, an event happened at Dartmoor, which ended in a very serious manner. A dispute arose between two of the prisoners late belonging to the United States' brig Argus, by the names of Thomas Hill and James Henry; the quarrel growing quite warm, and not being ended that night, they agreed to fight next morning; accordingly, next morning, about nine o'clock, they commenced the battle in prison No. 4, and by an unfortunate blow from Hill, Henry was killed on the spot; a jury of inquest was called next morning and held over the body of the deceased, and after hearing the evidence, the jury brought in a verdict of manslaughter, (or a killing not wholly without fault, but without malice.) Thomas Hill was removed and confined in the county prison at Exeter, there to await his trial at the August assizes then next ensuing.

The fourth of July now having arrived, and all things in great preparation, we displayed our flag in the yard, with the following inscription upon it in large capitals, "*All Canada or Dartmoor prison for life.*" This pleased the soldiers, but irritated the officers, who, discovering our firm resolution to defend the flag, and not having but part of a regiment in the garrison, and they friendly toward us, thought best to be quite silent, and let us proceed our own way; for if they attempted to deprive us of the flag, we might rush on the guard, who would make but a faint resistance, or join us, and all the prisoners might make an easy escape. But the prisoners did not wish to make the attempt, for they knew a reinforcement could easily be raised, and make a vigorous pursuit, and were therefore willing to wait some more favorable opportunity. At eleven o'clock all the prisoners assembled in the yard. The British officers belonging to the garrison, colonels, majors, captains, clerks, turnkeys, and a great number of soldiers, assembled on the walls to hear an oration composed by a Yankee sailor, upon the circumstances of the present times. An empty cask was placed in such a situation, as all the strangers on the walls could hear distinctly.

The orator of the day then mounted the cask, and all the spectators keeping a profound silence, began his oration, which we shall give our readers verbatim, as it was delivered by the sailor.

*Countrymen and fellow-citizens:*

This day we dedicate as the birth-day of freedom, it being the fourth of July—the day that our fathers declared themselves free and independent from the tyrannical laws of this country. After many years hard struggle, and the loss of many of our fathers and friends, America was acknowledged by all civilized nations, a free and independent government.

For many years our fathers, and we, their offspring, remained in the most perfect state of peace and tranquility, and reaped every blessing that grows on the soil of liberty; England, ever envying us the honor our fathers acquired by their valor in arms, when they declared that themselves and their sons should no longer wear the yoke of tyranny. Since that time, England has used every intrigue to deprive us of the greatest of blessings. First, contrary to the laws of civilized nations, she has dragged you from your homes, from your wives, your families and friends, into her infernal bulwarks—her ships of war; there, after suffering every degradation, from the terror of the lash, she has sent you to the most horrid prison in compensation for your long and faithful services. England, envying the happiness our countrymen enjoyed under so mild a government, the reverse of her own tyrannical laws, exerted every art to destroy their tranquility, by offering insults to the United States ships at various times, impressing and murdering our brother seamen, within the jurisdiction of our own waters, and within sight of our capitol. Our country was passive, and wishing to remain at peace with all nations, bore these insults with a fortitude becoming a great and wise people, and was in hope that, at some future day, England would redress those injuries in a fair and honorable way. But, contrary to every expectation for years before the war, she grew more bold, and showed a disposition to add injury to insult, by issuing orders to make prizes of all American vessels not bound to her own ports or those of her allies.

All nations stood amazed to see our country insulted, our seamen impressed and murdered within our own waters; our commerce confined and completely destroyed, contrary to the laws of neutrality. All this was done by England, and she unprovoked. Then, fellow-citizens, the results of all these depredations must be a formal declaration of war, which could no longer be delayed. Our country then, prudently and wisely, mustered all their forces, both by sea and land; England stood ready for combat fully prepared, and with the fullest assurance of a speedy victory; but, alas! for England; within a few weeks after the declaration of war, the United States frigate Constitution, commanded by Captain Isaac Hull, fell in with His Majesty's ship Guerriere, and then retaliated for one insult by sending her to the bottom. Great was the astonishment of England.

Shortly after, the U. S. ship Wasp fell in with His Majesty's ship Frolic, of far superior force, and after a second retaliation, she acknowledged her country's wrongs by striking her colors to the gallant Jones.

The officers and seamen of our infant navy now felt the ardor of our forefathers.

Decatur, in the frigate United States, fell in with a vessel of equal force, the Macedonian, the pride of the British navy; and, after displaying the courage of injured Americans, he took and brought her into port.

The Constitution shortly after took her station alongside of the Java, a frigate completely fitted and manned with a superior number of seamen; and again did the god of battle decide in favor of the injured Americans, and sent the Java to the bottom. The tidings had scarcely reached the American shore, when another laurel was added to our infant navy; the United States ship Hornet engaged His Majesty's ship Peacock, of equal force; and Capt. Lawrence, unwilling to make any distinction between her and the Java, sent her to the bottom, too.

This intelligence had scarcely reached the shores of liberty, when victories were proclaimed from all directions.

The British, feeling their pride wounded by the great exploits of our undaunted seamen, fitted out the Boxer, with the fullest assurance of recovering her lost honor, and were confident of taking our brig Enterprise, of much inferior force. But Divine Providence, ever extending the hand of assistance to the injured, decided the contest in favor of our insulted country; and the Boxer was captured and brought safe into port, in the United States.

Our next laurel was reaped on Lake Erie, by Commodore Perry. He bravely captured all the naval force on that lake, to the amazement of all surrounding nations, and the disgrace of the British flag.

Commodore Chauncey, at the same time, had a complete ascendency over the whole British force on Lake Ontario; while Commodore Rodgers is traversing the ocean in every direction, and destroying British property to an immense value. The United States ship Essex is complete master of all the South Seas, in defiance of all the boasted superiority of the British. The United States ship Congress is cruising on the coast of Brazil, and completely intercepting the trade of Great Britain to all Spanish South America, and defying any thing of equal size.

And now, fellow-citizens, this country, what has she done? She has long boasted of her honor and her bravery; and she has issued orders to her frigates, never to engage an American frigate unless under cover of a ship of the line. She has likewise endeavored to rouse the anger of the savage tribes in the wilderness of Canada, to murder and scalp your brethren in arms, in that country. But Divine Providence, still assisting your injured country, turned the ferocity of the savages against those who moved them to anger, and their vengeance recoiled on the hand that attempted to use it. And you, fellow-citizens, although prisoners of war, feel the benefit of belonging to so great and wise a nation. Have the United States not assisted us in our unhappy situation, and much meliorated our sufferings, though illy able while carrying on so expensive a war?

And now, fellow-citizens, I conjure you to be patient, and consider your country to be using her utmost endeavor to bring about an honorable and speedy peace. In a state of war, many stories are circulated in this country favorable to her success in arms, which have no foundation; and this is done to encourage and inspire the soldiery to enlist in her wars; and perhaps, fellow-citizens, many of you may honestly believe the reports, but let them not make you despair of your country. No, depend upon it, she cannot be conquered. England may get momentary possession of one small city, or perhaps ten, but America is not conquered till every man is either taken prisoner or killed.

The success of our naval arms is a sufficient proof, and our country is now in triumph at her great naval success. Have we not this moment, as it were, heard of another brilliant achievement upon the ocean? The United States ship Peacock, on her first cruise after she left the stocks, captured and brought into port His Majesty's ship L'Epervier, of equal size, with immense sums of silver and much treasure on board?

From the success of American arms, which have already astonished our enemies, we have nothing to fear; and we have the greatest reason to believe that the American cause is big with the most wonderful achievements; that the exploits of our countrymen in arms, in the present contest, will astonish all nations, and be recorded on the pages of history, and remain in the choicest archives of posterity, with equal glory to those of Marathon and Thermopylæ.

Fellow-prisoners, let us then be resigned to our present unhappy condition; and through the great exertion of our country, and the assistance of Divine Providence, who disposes of events and governs futurity, we may hope once more to revisit our native country in an honorable peace, and live happy and free.

After the oration was delivered, the officers that were on the walls entered the prison yard, and expressed the greatest surprise that we should entertain a hope that the United States would be successful in a war with Great Britain, when she was at peace with all other nations. But for *consolation* to us in our present condition, we might rest fully assured that we should be released in a very short time by a peace, which would be brought about by their conquering the United States, and reducing them to colonies again; and such a change, which must shortly take place, they said must be imputed entirely to the bad management of our President and Congress: we have now conquered France, and America must be conquered next. We found them ignorant of the strength and resources of the American people; we gave them a particular account of the situation of America, her means of defence, and the spirit and determination of the people; the great superiority of gunnery which the American seamen possessed over those of Great Britain; the truth of which was shown in the actions of the Guerriere, Frolic, Java, &c., &c.

They left the yard much chagrined at these facts, which they could not deny; and remarking that they were surprised to find sailors so well acquainted with the politics of both countries, but that they believed they must be most of them Englishmen born, and that it was a very great pity His Majesty should be deprived of so many valuable seamen.

At two o'clock we sat down to our fourth of July dinner, which was composed of soup and beef, the best we could prepare. We gathered in parties, with the greatest animation, conversing of our President and Congress, for whom we sailors have the greatest respect; and Mr. Madison, particularly, is a great favorite of sailors. After dinner we had a song, which was composed for the occasion.

The day was passed in the greatest harmony; no quarrel or strife occurred to mar its pleasure. The next day every man resumed his occupation, and seemed to enjoy a negative happiness, which arose from a freedom from absolute pain.

On the eighth of this month, a friend of mine, for whom I had much respect, died; and at his burial I took occasion to survey the vast tenements of the dead, and consider, within myself, what innumerable multitudes of people lay confused together on this moor; how friends and enemies, officers and soldiers, the brave and the coward, collected from all quarters of the globe, of all nations, and of all colors, lay undistinguished in one common mass of matter; and not a stone to name one tenant of the tomb.

After having surveyed this great magazine of mortality as it were, in the lump, out of respect to my friend, I searched about and obtained a very slaty stone, on which I inscribed the following words:

Here lies the body of

JAMES HART,

A native of the United States of

America,

*Who departed this life July 8th, 1814.*

Under which was the following epitaph:

Your country mourns your hapless fate;

So mourn we prisoners all;

You've paid the debt we all must pay,

Each sailor, great and small.

Your body on this barren moor,—

Your soul in Heaven doth rest,

Where Yankee sailors, one and all,

Hereafter will be blest.

The agent permitted us to put this stone up, and of the many thousands that lay indiscriminately mingled together upon this moor, this stone recorded the only syllable of the dead buried here. The life of these men is finely described in Holy Writ by the path of an arrow, which is immediately closed up and lost.

We received our monthly pay as usual, and nothing remarkable occurred during the remainder of the month; few persons arrived, but we had expectation of a great number. The weather was rainy and cold; the prisoners generally healthy; few died, but the prison was very much crowded, there being 1,500 in No. 4.

At the commencement of August, a draft of prisoners arrived, who had been recently captured on the coast of Europe, among whom were four men lately belonging to the private armed schooner Surprise, of Baltimore; these four men, on their first arrival at this depot, were put into close confinement in the cachot, there to remain on two-thirds allowance, without hammock or bed, sleeping on the stone floor, during their whole imprisonment. When the cause of their confinement was known, it seems it had grown out of the following circumstances:

The Surprise was cruising in the channel of England, and fell in with, and captured, a schooner, and put on board her these four men, to take charge of the prize.

Shortly after, the prize was recaptured by an English frigate, and, after taking possession of her, found stowed away in the round-house (which is a few feet above the deck) a cask of powder, which contained but a few pounds at most, and on examination they found part of a match and a candle; the captain of the frigate, being suspicious of these four men's having an intention to blow the vessel up, took them and committed them to close confinement until he arrived in England; he then reported them to the Board of Transport, and delivered them into their custody, and they, from these suspicious circumstances, sentenced them to the punishment above mentioned. Whether the crime, had it been well proved, would warrant so rigorous a punishment, is not the subject of investigation; they had the power to treat them as they pleased, nor had the sufferers any redress, for, *inter armis lages silent*, "the laws are silent amid arms."

On the arrival of these prisoners, Capt. Shortland opened the south yard of the enclosure, and gave all the officers liberty to go into No. 6. A few days after, a *habeas corpus ad testificandum* was awarded to bring forward six prisoners, to appear and give evidence in the cause of Thomas Hill, then depending at the next Exeter assizes, who was charged with manslaughter for killing James Henry on the third of July. The termination of the trial, I shall give in a subsequent page.

The prisoners having no expectation or hope of exchange, or a peace, now set about contriving a method of escape, something of which we hinted at in a preceding page. The plan was to dig out of prison No. 6. The plan was made known to the prisoners in No. 4, who were expecting to be removed into No. 6 in a few days, when they would have access to Nos. 5, 6, and 7, which were contained in one yard. To have the plan circulated with the greatest secrecy that would obtain the opinion of all the prisoners, without the suspicion of the guards or officers, it was thought best to have it done in poetry, and accordingly it was done in that manner. This attracted the attention of the prisoners, and we soon found the intention of each man to favor the plan.

On the fifteenth of August, the six men whom we mentioned in the preceding page, were taken to Exeter, returned, and with them Thomas Hill, who was acquitted by the jury, and he remanded to Dartmoor as a prisoner of war.

The same day arrived a large draft of prisoners, who had been sent from Halifax prison on board the transport ship Bensen. These persons, on their passage, attempted to rise and take the ship, in which attempt a sharp contest ensued, and the struggle was for some time doubtful, but the American prisoners were overpowered, and afterwards treated with the greatest severity and cruelty. In the engagement several on both sides were severely wounded, but none killed or mortally wounded. Some of the prisoners were taken out and put on board the ship Commodore, and the remainder confined in the coal-hole, and kept on bread and water for several days.

These prisoners were put into No. 6, which now made about eight hundred in that prison, and about twelve hundred in No. 4, who were not yet removed.

We finding our number increasing daily, and no prospect of peace or exchange, now determined to put in execution our projected plan of escape; every prisoner being willing, and not a dissenting voice among the whole, we mustered a number of bibles in each prison, and began to solemnly swear every man to keep secret every transaction he should see or know of concerning the operation then about to be begun; when a man was sworn, he was strictly cautioned and charged not to make known, by word or sign, in any way whatever, anything which might lead to a discovery of their design, on pain of immediate death in a private and secret manner, which would most assuredly take place without the knowledge of the keepers.

After they were all sworn, and the fixed determination of hanging the first informer, a number of confidential persons were appointed as spies, to watch the conduct of others. We also appointed other trusty men to watch the movements of the turnkeys and sentries, and see that the prisoners held no conversation with either of them. We then divided ourselves into parties to work, and who were alternately to dig and relieve each other.

After taking a correct survey of the ground, measuring and making it out, and taking the course, on the twentieth we made a beginning in both prisons, and dug directly down. In this perpendicular direction we must sink our work twenty feet, which would come on a horizontal plane with the road. On this horizontal plane we must then pursue the work, in an eastern direction, two hundred and fifty feet, which distance would carry us beyond the outer wall and under all the foundations which extended below the surface of the earth about six feet; if this work were performed we should then have a passage into the road. The digging could be carried on with very little difficulty: but the great obstacle before us was to convey away the dirt, and this, on a little consideration, seemed to vanish when we considered the stream of water in the yard, which passed under the prison at the rate of four miles an hour; into this stream we threw great quantities of fine dirt, which passed off. We, as another means to get clear of the dirt, obtained permission to bring into the prison a large quantity of lime, under the pretence of white-washing the walls of the prison.

These walls were made of large rough stone, and every night we made of the dirt a sort of morter, and plastered on the walls, and then white-washed it over.

No. 5 prison containing no prisoners, and not being visited by the keepers, we thought best to begin a similar operation in that prison, as we could pass and repass into it unknown to the keepers. In this we commenced digging in the day-time, and found a hollow place under the prison to stow the dirt away.

In these three different places we made our attacks, and very rightly supposing, that if one should be discovered, that we should still have another, which we could proceed in without suspicion; we were apprehensive that the run of water, which passed through an iron grating at the outlet, might get stopped with the dirt, and lead to a discovery. We hastened on the work, every man as busy as a bee, and flushed with the hope and full belief that we should shortly make our escape.

At the close of the month, we had dug toward the wall in a horizontal direction forty feet, without the least suspicion. As we entered so far under ground we found a want of fresh air, and to remedy this, we contrived a lamp to keep burning in the hole, that would expel all the axotic gas, or dead air, and bring in a constant supply of fresh.

I must digress for a moment, to give an account of some events which took place during this operation.

In the meanwhile a number of prisoners arrived; some from Chatham, some from the West Indies, and from other places. These, as soon as they arrived, were made acquainted with our design and operations, and sworn and charged as the others had been. Among these prisoners was the crew of the United States brig Frolic. These prisoners were destitute of clothing, and in a very bad state of health, which was occasioned by being so very closely confined during the passage, and their allowance so very short. During the month we had great quantities of rain, which was very favorable to our operations. The prisoners were now more healthy than they had been before since our confinement. Those who had been sick for some time died. Those who had been here a long time had become used to the hardships, but new comers were sickly.

On the last day of August, our subterraneous passage was sixty feet from No. 5, and about the same from No. 6, and No. 4 nearly equal. The dirt being very loose, and but few stones to obstruct our way, our passage seemed short, and promised success.

September having commenced, and no suspicion or discovery as yet made, although the prisons were searched every day by the keepers; but the holes being very small, and so nicely closed every day, that it would require the minutest search to discover the place; but the hole was larger under ground, and would admit four men to work abreast.

But, to our great mortification, on the second, Capt. Shortland entered the prison with the guards, and went directly towards the hole, and as he passed, he informed us that he knew of our operations in No. 5, but his informer had not told him correctly, for after a long search, they could not discover the hole.

It was then suggested by his attendants to sound the prison; they then began with crow-bars to sound, and after having made the minutest examination, by accident found the entrance, to the great mortification of every man.

They undertook to enter the hole, but after entering a few feet, their lights went out, and they could not keep them burning; and being unacquainted with the materials, and method used by us to light the hole and expel the dead air, could not penetrate to the extent, nor did they ever enter near all the distance.

They were no less astonished to conceive what had become of the dirt taken from the passage, and it ever remained a great mystery to them.

Every man was strictly cautioned, should any discovery take place, not to give any account whatever of the means they had made use of to light the hole, or how they had disposed of the dirt; and when they were strictly examined by the officers, they gave no other answer, than that each man eat his proportion, to make up his scant allowance.

To prevent any further operation of this kind, Capt. Shortland had every prisoner removed from the yard which encloses No. 5, 6, and 7, into the enclosure on the north side, which contained No. 1, 2, and 3; but having no suspicions of any attempts to escape in No. 4, they let the prisoners there remain.

After the prisoners were removed from the other two prisons, they filled the entrance of the hole up with stone: they supposed these were not eatable.

We remained in No. 2 till the eighth, when we were again removed to the south side, on account of prison No. 2 being out of repair. This gave us fresh hopes. As the noise had not yet entirely got silent, we thought best to stop all operations in No. 4 for the present.

In the mean while, our court of judicature was sitting, and several persons were arraigned at the bar, and charged with having given information of our design to escape; all the evidence against them was produced, but the crime being of a capital nature by our laws, required positive and direct evidence, which the court considered had not been produced; and although very strong circumstantial evidence had been given, yet they considered that such evidence ought never to take a man's life, which must have been the case had any one been found guilty.

We afterwards believed it must have been accidental; that some person had spoken too loud, or in an unguarded manner in the presence of the turnkeys; for we found no discovery had been made of the operations in No. 4 or 5, although Capt. Shortland had declared himself to be acquainted with them in No. 5.

After the bustle of the discovery had a little blown over, and the officers and keepers had ridiculed the futile idea of our making our escape, by saying they had guards and spies in all directions; we then gave orders to the blacks in No. 4 to proceed on with their work. At this time, the 10th, a draft of prisoners arrived from Chatham; these were mostly men delivered up from ships of war in England, and some few were sent from the West Indies, Bermuda, and New Providence.—This draft increased the number of prisoners at this depot to three thousand five hundred in all.

When these men arrived, we were under great apprehensions that they would be ordered into No. 5, and in the hurry and bustle of entering, before they were cautioned, might lead to a discovery of the work in that prison; but happily, they were ordered into No. 7, and all the white prisoners from No. 4 ordered in with them; and all the blacks were now to be kept by themselves.

They were directed to proceed as we mentioned before, and to report progress every evening. As the hole in No. 6 was farthest advanced, we formed a communication to let each other know their progress each day, that all the holes might proceed with equal progress, and come out at the same time.

With this arrangement we proceeded on, and on the 12th, in No. 6, we dug down, and the next day had gone quite round the stones which were thrown in to fill up the entrance of the hole, and came out into the former passage: this was done in the night, and in the day time we carried on the work in No. 5, disposing of the dirt as before.

The work went on with the greatest care, secrecy and success, and every man was animated with the liveliest hope of soon gaining his liberty, till each hole had come within thirty-five or forty feet of the intended place of coming out.

We could always ascertain the distance we were from the top of the ground by measuring with our line and rule, and had concluded to work that distance in one week: every man was now provided with a dagger, made by prisoners who worked at black-smithing.

When the work was complete, we were to make our move some dark stormy night at the hour of ten, which would give every man who wished, an opportunity to reach Torbay, about ten miles distant, at which place lay a large number of unarmed vessels, fishing boats and other small craft; we could reach this place a little after midnight, and then proceed as fast as possible for France; on leaving the outlet of the passage every man was to separate and take care of himself. When we were once out, we had determined to reach France or sell our lives at the dearest rate; for, by this time, life was of little consequence to us, when we compared it to the miseries we must suffer, if we should be brought back, and therefore we were determined to hazard it at all events.

But I hasten from our future resolutions to relieve the reader from his anxiety, by showing the event.

At this moment, when every man was well pleased with the prospect, how was his just indignation raised, and his fierce anger kindled!—a man by the name of [1]Bagley, another Sinon, walked out in the open day, before all the prisoners then in the yard, went up to the turnkeys and marched off with them to the keeper's house, gave him information of all the operations and designs, and we never saw him after; for could we have catched him, we should scarcely have tried him, but should have torn him in atoms before the life could have time to leave his traitorous body.

This Judas received the price of his iniquity from the Transport Board, and got a passport to go where he pleased, and the public's humble servant put into the cachot;—but I can tell him, should this work ever reach his infamous hand, that it is the sincere wish of every prisoner, that he may fall, and like that other Judas, his bowels may gush out.

The prisoners were then immediately removed to the north side of the enclosure, and confined to No. 1 and 3; and to repair the damages which had been done to the prisons, Capt. Shortland put every man on two thirds allowance, and took the other third to pay expenses of repair; this he did for ten days successively; if we had eaten the dirt up, we had to starve it back again.

Our hopes were all blown up to the moon, and we left to despair; we had no prospect by which we could hope to be relieved, but every thing seemed to threaten us with imprisonment for life. We again resigned ourselves to our situation, and placed all our hopes of life and liberty on that Almighty arm, which had brought us to these sufferings by His Divine pleasure. Every man with reluctance now returns to his usual occupation, hoping to gain a few articles of clothing, which he stood in need of. The shoes furnished by Mr. Beasley, which were the poorest that could be made in England, were now worn out, and we needed others.

It was reported among the prisoners, that an exchange was about to take place; but as we had no account to that effect from Mr. Beasley, we could place no dependence on it; the only hope we had was bribing the guards, and that of peace.

By letters from Plymouth, we had information that an action had been fought between the Essex, Capt. Porter, and the British frigate Phebe, Capt. Hillyar, and a sloop of war. The action was long and severe, and much blood spilt on both sides; and although the Essex was taken, the honour of the day belonged to the Americans. She fought under every disadvantage, and gallantly stood the fire of both the enemy's vessels, and bore hard for a victory, till chance decided against her. The magnanimity of the officers and crew commands the noblest sentiments of respect from every American; they deserved no common meed of praise; I therefore undertook to celebrate their valorous deeds in verse.

A large draft of prisoners, from Chatham, arrived at this place the latter end of this month; among them were great numbers of men who had been detained on board His Majesty's ships from eight to twelve years, and one who had been detained eighteen years. The greatest part of this draft were men who had been delivered up from the navy; they were collected at Chatham, and brought round by water to Plymouth, landed, and then ordered to prepare to march for Dartmoor prison, the sufferings of which they had long been acquainted with, by report; but previous to their departure, they, anticipating their treatment there, prepared the following motto, in capitals, and fixed it to the fore part of their hats: "*British gratitude for past services.*" With this on their hats, they marched the distance of eighteen miles. During the march, the officers tried every means to persuade them to take it off, but they absolutely refused, saying it was truth, and, as prisoners of war, they had a just cause to complain of the treatment and ingratitude of a government which they had so long served. They insisted that it was cruelty to make them prisoners, after they had served so many years as good and faithful servants; and it was much more ungrateful now to send them to the worst prison in England, as a compensation for their long and faithful services.

The garrison was now reinforced by a large number of soldiers, and the prisoners separated; the whites in the north and south wing, occupying two prisons in each yard, and the blacks one in the centre. The prisoners were not permitted to have intercourse with one another from the different prisons, except on Sundays.

The number being now very large, it was feared they would rise, and take possession of the guard-house, and then make their escape. They had some ground to fear the event might take place, for the prisoners did not consider these walls, nor the soldiers, any very great obstacle in the accomplishment of such an undertaking, had it been their design. But they knew very well the consequence of doing this; although, on the first *sortie*, the officers, soldiers and guards, must fall into their power, yet as the prisoners must all march in a body to keep them under, the alarm would spread over all England, and the militia be raised upon them, before they would be able to reach the sea-coast and take shipping.

Capt. Shortland was in daily fear of such an attack, for there was scarce a day but some dispute or strife took place between the turnkeys or guards and the prisoners, and kept a continual alarm. The prisoners would not hear any abusive language against the President of the United States; and on the first disrespectful word from a sentry, stationed singly in the yard, they would knock him down, and he could get no relief till they were willing to release him, for the prisoners immediately surrounded him by hundreds; and the garrison declared that they had more trouble with four thousand Americans than they should have with twenty thousand Frenchmen.

On the last day of this month, another draft arrived, among whom were the crew of the United States brig Rattlesnake and some others, sent from Halifax.

The prisoners became sickly again, and upwards of one hundred in the hospital; but they had much better attendance than before, having now a new surgeon, Dr. Magrath, to superintend that department; he was a humane, skilful and attentive man, and a friend to the sick and distressed prisoner. I know of nothing more agreeable to the human feelings than the presence of a friend by our sick-bed; and this man administered more of the medicine of life by the sympathetic emotions of his heart than all the anodynes in the apothecary's shop.

We had much rain and stormy weather during the month of September. One tedious month had now passed by, and another lay in hopeless prospect before us; but our hopes were a little revived on the second of October by a letter which we received from Mr. Beasley, informing us that a partial exchange would take place between the two countries. This exchange would extend to none but those taken in the United States vessels; this letter was to inform the crew of the Argus more particularly, as they were the oldest prisoners taken in the United States service. The same letter gave general information that there was great prospects of a speedy peace between the two belligerents.

*Several persons made their escape by bribing the sentries after this news,* and passing out in the night, with a soldier's coat and cap on, under his protection. But this method was discovered and stopped, and eight only were able to make their escape by it.

We received the account of the United States ship Wasp sinking the Reindeer and Avon. The particulars seemed too galling to their feelings to publish. After reading the account in the London paper, I composed a dirge, and put it up on the front of the prison, in full sight of all the soldier-officers and guards, as a tribute of respect to departed worthies of His Majesty's navy.

Almost every draft of prisoners brought intelligence of new victories of the Americans by sea, and every British paper was filled with complaints of American privateers destroying British property in their own waters, and in sight of their cities. The prisoners, being animated with the success of the arms of their country, could not forbear expressing their joy in some pleasant feat. The following anecdote has something of the features of the attack of Don Quixotte on the wind-mill. The prisoners, the night after the news of the Wasp, took a jacket at twelve at night, lowered it down towards the ground along the rope of the prison; the soldiers saw it, and concluded it must be a man sliding down the rope to make his escape; the alarm was given, and Capt. Shortland and all the soldier-officers at the head of the picket, entered, and hailed the man on the rope, but no answer; they then drew themselves up in martial array, and every man sat his teeth and screwed his courage up to the sticking place, ready for battle; Capt. Shortland, an experienced officer, gave orders to fire, and instantly a volley of musketry was poured in upon the enemy, and down came the jacket; they rushed in upon it, and, to their astonishment, they had conquered a jacket.

The keepers who had been so insolent the day before, by wishing Mr. Madison in the prison, now showed great resentment, and gave themselves many airs upon the occasion. The soldiers discovered a candle burning in the prison, and called aloud, "put out that candle;" but the order not being instantly obeyed, they discharged a volley through the window; but a divine interposition of goodness seemed to direct the balls, for every one lodged in some part of the hammocks, which almost formed a solid column, and not a single man hurt or touched, though asleep in the hammocks. The next morning I thought the battle with the jacket and the attack on the sleeping prisoners deserved to be celebrated in some signal way, and sung like the deeds of the gallant Quixotte.

It had been remarked by the prisoners that, about the time of some reverse of the arms of the enemy, the keepers treated them with much greater severity, and seemed to wish to wreak their vengeance in retaliation on the prisoners.

On the eighteenth, orders, together with a list of names, came to discharge sixty-two of the crew of the late United States brig Frolic, who had been exchanged, and were to repair immediately to Dartmouth, thirty miles from the depot, to go on board the cartel Janey, then lying at that place with the greater part of her number, which consisted of prisoners late belonging to the United States navy and army.

Those sixty-two of the Frolic were obliged to carry the baggage themselves or leave it behind, for they were allowed no means to transport it. Twelve miles of the distance is water carriage; the other eighteen is land—this distance they had to march on foot; they received a shilling each man, and one day's provision, at the commencement of the journey.

By letters from Plymouth, we received intelligence that another cartel, the St. Philip, was preparing to take on board part of her complement at that place, then to proceed to Dartmouth, and receive the crew of the late United States brig Argus, and her officers, and non-combatants from Ashburton. The same letters informed us that all the prisoners in England, then nearly five thousand, would shortly be removed to this prison; and, accordingly, at the latter end of this month they all were removed to this depot, and made, with some few lately from sea, five thousand and twenty. They were badly prepared to stand the inclemency of the approaching season; they were all miserably clothed, and the shoes they had received from Mr. Beasley lasted but a few weeks, and they were now quite destitute and very sickly, and the weather cold and stormy for several days together. On the third we received a letter from Mr. Beasley, informing us that his clerk, Mr. Williams, was on his way from London to this place with clothing, which he would distribute among the prisoners captured since the middle of last May, and to those captured before that date he would deliver one shirt and one pair of shoes and stockings, which should be their supply for nine months. The old prisoners stated their situation to Mr. Beasley, by letter, at the same date, and informed him that they were in need of clothing; that what they received in May was worn out, also their shoes, and that they were not supplied with sufficient bedding to make them any way comfortable through the approaching winter, especially as they were sickly, and had the small-pox in the prison, and that they should not be able to endure the hardships of their condition, though their two and a half pence a day was some relief; yet as all the workmen were turned into prison, and not permitted to go out any more on account of one man, whom we believe to be Capt. Swain, of New Bedford, Massachusetts, taking a very sudden move and leaving the whole establishment without giving notice; this left them unprovided with sufficient means to take care of themselves.

Now the surly blasts of chill November had made all surrounding nature wear the sad aspect of decay, and the barefooted prisoner stood shivering by the walls, in the pale and feeble ray of a winter sun, when Mr. Williams arrived with the clothing, as was expected, and on the third saw the crew of the Argus take their departure from this prison, to go on board the St. Philip, then lying at Dartmouth, bound for the United States. The draft of this crew consisted of one hundred, which was all that was taken from this place; she had previously taken in her complement, except this number, at Chatham. Shortly after her sailing from Dartmouth she was so unfortunate as to spring her mast, and obliged to return into port.

At this time the Phebe and the late United States frigate Essex arrived in England. The editors who published the arrival of these two ships, made no remark or observation whatever, only barely said they had arrived.

The reader will not have forgotten the circumstance of the four men, whom we mentioned were committed to close confinement during the war, on suspicion of an intention to blow up the ship. We, at this time, made application to the Board of Transport, to mitigate the punishment of these four men, late of the Surprise, and who had remained ever since in close confinement in the cachot, but our petition was not granted; the board said the sentence had passed and could not be recalled—they must suffer according to the sentence. These poor fellows had endured the three months imprisonment with a magnanimity becoming Americans. The prisoners seeing they could not get them relieved, agreed to allow them a halfpenny a month out of every man's pay, which was cheerfully done by every man. They supplied them with such articles as the board would allow them to have.

Our hope now brightened amidst the clouds of sufferings and despair, by the reports from Ghent of a speedy peace, which swelled every London paper.

The guards, both officers and soldiers, stationed here, were much disaffected with the government of the country; and informed us that the military through the whole kingdom had the same disaffection, and that they had gone so far as to inform the government, in direct terms, that if a peace did not take place before the first of April, that they would lay down their arms.

The battle and destruction of Washington had now crossed the Atlantic, and was sounding with great applause to the British arms; every paper was swelled with the most pompous description of the great battle, and the unparalleled bravery and magnanimity of their officers and soldiers, that had defeated and drove the whole American army, headed by Mr. Madison in person, and that they were in so close pursuit of him that he had a severe race all the way from Bladensburgh to Washington, which they were disposed to ridicule by comparing to John Gilpin's celebrated race.

They also gave a description of Washington, which they declared was one of the greatest cities in the known world; the grandeur and magnificence of it surpassed that of Paris or London; it contained thirteen hundred spacious squares. But they did not mention that those squares contained no houses or inhabitants.

These stories could not gain the belief of persons acquainted with the American nation and its capitol, but we were led to believe that the conduct on both sides deserved much censure, and that the burning of that capitol was a disgrace to both nations.

Nothing very material occurred among the prisoners this month; they received their monthly pay as usual, but were more sickly, and the weather cold and tedious, but could not be compared with the November before. The prisoners, though far from being as comfortable as they ought to be, suffered much less, and were in a better condition to endure the hardships of a prison than the year before, now they were supplied with one pair of shoes and stockings, and allowed two and a half pence per day. They did not shrink at the approaching season so much as before.

Mr. Williams returned to London at the end of the month; he had been with us all the month, distributing the several articles above mentioned.

As the season advanced the hard weather increased, and the snow fell in great abundance in the beginning of December, and the prisoners, much chilled with the cold, applied for permission to keep fire, as had been permitted to the French prisoners, but were peremptorily refused and absolutely forbid.

But to make the best of these evils of life, they applied themselves every man to some occupation; they endeavored to cherish and keep the mind alive if the body decayed, and to cultivate that nobler part of our being, they established a number of schools, and the young men and boys were instructed in them for nearly two years, and many of them, who were perfectly unacquainted with letters when they came to this prison, had acquired a tolerable education in the English branches of science.

There has, from the earliest ages of antiquity, been frequent instances of men who have been weary of life, and had not the courage and fortitude to bear those ills which are incident to it, and have, therefore, by a sort of false heroism, attempted to avoid them by destroying their own life. The Stoic philosophy, which seemed to be a cultivated degree of insensibility, encouraged it, and called it heroism; but the act is cowardly, and a great offence against the laws of God and man.

I have thought proper to premise these observations, before I related the melancholy instance of a young man, a native of the city of New York, by the name of John Taylor, who put an end to his life on the first of this month, by hanging himself, in prison No. 5.

By the position in which he was found in the morning, he must have been all intent on death; he had fastened himself to one of the stantions so that his toes could just touch the floor. We knew of no other cause than that despair had given him less courage to live than to die.

Thinking it might tend to deter others from following the example of this unhappy victim of despair, I procured a large slate, and engraved on it the following inscription, which I put at the head of his grave, where it remains on the moor:

Here lies

JOHN TAYLOR,

A native citizen of the city of New York,

Who committed suicide, by hanging himself

in prison No. 5, on the evening

of the first of December, 1814.

I then put over each prison, as a *caveat*, the following *memento*, as it was feared others would do the same act:

Whene'er you view this doleful tomb,

Remember what you are,

And put your trust in God alone:

Suppress that fiend, Despair.

Lo! there's entomb'd a generous youth

Despair did doom to die;

By the hard act of suicide,

John Taylor there doth lie.

He hung himself within yon walls,—

A warning may it prove:

Tho' man is wicked here below,

There's a just God above.


Be patient, meek, and wait His call,

Endure these ills of strife:

For great's the sin of mortal man,

That takes away his life.


One knows not how to account for the origin of that act which takes away one's own life: self-love and self-preservation are so deeply rooted in the very nature of all living creatures, that it is the ultimate motive of all actions to endeavor to sustain and preserve life; fear of destroying it is so instinctive in all animals that they seem to flee from danger without any reasoning in the act, and almost without knowing when the volition begins.

But the suicide reverses everything; he does an act which is not natural, not rational, not desirable, and dangerous; he rushes into the presence of his God with all his former crimes, and this most heinous of all brings him there.

From the first to the twenty-sixth nothing material occurred, but a constant fall of snow every day; but the season was less severe than that of the year before.

In the interim, prisoners arrived from different quarters of the globe; some taken in Canada on the lakes, and others on the land; and amongst these arrivals was the crew of the privateer Leo, captured off the coast of Portugal.

On the twenty-ninth, we were most agreeably surprised with the joyful tidings of peace! The preliminaries were announced in the London paper which we received this day, and the news was confirmed by a letter from Mr. Beasley, received the same day, stating that the treaty had been signed by the Commissioners at Ghent, on the 24th, and that the sloop-of-war Favorite would sail with the treaty on the second of January, one thousand eight hundred and fifteen, with all possible speed, for the United States, and that three months would release every man from confinement.

Language is too feeble to describe the transports of joy that so suddenly and unexpectedly filled every heart. Every man forgot the many tedious days and nights he had so often numbered over within these prison walls. The memory of his better days rose fresh in his mind, and he once more hoped to return to his native country, which he had so long despaired of ever revisiting; his liberty, the embraces of his friends, he knew better how to prize by being so long deprived of them. The delicious fruits of plenty he could by his imagination taste.

The prison was now in great confusion and bustle in preparing to celebrate the peace, which we were confident would be honorable to our country. We were confident that the ground-work of the treaty must be free trade and sailors' rights, and made arrangements to celebrate it in a manner conformable to the rights of the ocean.

We obtained a quantity of powder of the soldiers, unknown to the keepers, and made large cartridges, wound them up in twine, so that when exploded would make a report as loud as a six-pounder; we then procured a large ensign, and a pendant for each prison; we prepared a white flag in the centre, painted in large capitals, "FREE TRADE AND SAILORS' RIGHTS."

The next morning, to the astonishment of the officers and guards, we displayed the flags on the top of each prison; and on No. 3, which was styled the Commodore, displayed the white flag with the above motto, and at the same time fired a salute of seventeen rounds.

Shortly after, Capt. Shortland entered the yard, and politely requested the white flag, containing the motto, to be taken down, as it would draw censure upon him from the government, by holding out inducements for the sailors to mutinise; he said the government of Great Britain took care to suppress all such inflammatory mottoes. But the prisoners were too full of spirits to comply with the request at that time. They continued it till towards evening, when he again entered and solicited us to take it down, or everything would be in confusion; he said if we would take the motto-flag down, he would hoist an American ensign on one end of his own house, and a British one on the other end; and if we were not contented with this he would order them all down; we then told him, out of respect for him, we would take them all down, and wait till the ratification of peace before we displayed them again.

On the thirty-first of this month arrived a draft of prisoners, among whom were many who had given themselves up as American citizens, and claimed their right to a citizenship, and refused to act on board his Majesty's ships any longer; these the prisoners did not give a very welcome reception, for they had delayed till the act had become a wilful aiding and assisting the enemy, and the mischief now over. The constant cry among the sailors, who are great friends to Uncle Sam, was, "Damn my eyes if he han't stood it like a man."

Among those prisoners who had declared themselves citizens of the United States, were six who had been in the enemy's service for many years, and were on board His Majesty's ship Pelican when she engaged the United States brig Argus, and took a very active part in the action against the Argus; every man of them had been appointed to some petty office on board the Pelican. But, supposing a peace would shortly be concluded between the two nations, they had thought best to claim a citizenship, and obtain their release. This information soon spread among all the prisoners, and enraged them to the highest degree at their conduct; and being flushed with high spirits with the late news of peace, were about to proceed to extremities with them, and they, finding their lives were in danger, applied to Capt. Shortland for protection, who entered the prison yard with guards and took these traitorous villains along, and we believe they went back into his Majesty's service, as the next day they were conveyed to Plymouth, and we heard no more of them.

The weather was now very severe, and the oldest prisoners had not received any clothing since May, and were much in need of jackets and trowers, of this fact the prisoners were a self-evident and naked truth. Many were sick in the hospital.

December thirty-first, 1814. Statement of prisoners in prison at this depot:

Prisoners delivered up from the British navy,                    1978

United States' and privateers' men, those taken in merchant vessels, 3348

_____

Total, exclusive of those exchanged,                    5326

Mr. Beasley, agent, had visited them once. They had received from him one jacket, one pair of trowsers, two shirts, two pair of shoes, and two pair of stockings, each man.

Received from the British government, one hammock, one blanket, one horse rug, one bed, one yellow jacket, one pair of trowers, one waistcoat, one pair of wooden shoes, and one cap.

Received in cash one and a half pence, to which was added one penny more after two months, each man per day, from the first of January, 1814.

The weather still continued cold, and the oldest prisoners had not as yet received any shoes or clothes, but were daily expecting them from Mr. Beasley.

We had been in this cold and dreary mansion twenty-one months, and the above items were all the assistance we had received from Beasley, the only person in this foreign land of our enemies to whom we could look for any assistance, or from whom we had any right to expect it.

Our ears had been constantly assailed with the groans of the sick and the dying; pestilence and disease had been our constant companions; our minds had become almost distracted betwixt the grief for our departed friends and fellow-prisoners and the hunger and want of our own body. From such a long series of incessant sufferings, it is natural to suppose that the bodies were emaciated and the mind debilitated; and much of the sameness that may appear in this narrative is owing to a uniform state of misery, which will not admit of a variety in the description.

Capt. Shortland had got information on the second of November, 1815, that the prisoners had counterfeited three shilling pieces, and passed them to the market people, for their country produce, and shortly after he detected two men attempting to pass bad money; he had them apprehended immediately, and sent to the cachot.

Nothing worthy of note occurred till the twentieth, when two men lately arrived were discovered to be the same who had entered the British service the winter before. After having received many insults, and much hard usage, on board the war ships, they had got tired of their situations, and claimed their citizenship and got themselves delivered up and sent to prison again, which they considered the least of the two evils.

Their conduct on board the ships, was no doubt as disgraceful as the act they committed to bring them there; they shifted from ship to ship, till the one wherein they claimed their citizenship was ignorant of the manner they had come into the service. The prisoners being highly enraged at such conduct, made strict inquiry into the matter, and found the facts as above mentioned.—After holding consultations, many were for putting them to immediate death, others were for flogging them as severely as they could bear, and every man for giving them some condign punishment; but at last it was unanimously concluded to put upon them a mark, which would be a lasting stigma, and an example for others. They seized and took the traitors into prison, and fastened them to a table, so that they could not resist, and then, with needles and India ink, pricked U. S. on one cheek, and T. on the other; which is United States Traitor. After we let them go, they were taken immediately to the hospital, and their faces blistered on both sides, to endeavor to extract the ink, but this only made it brighter and sink deeper in. The doctors reported the traitors to be in a very dangerous state, and that their lives were despaired of. If this had been the case, it must only proceed from the application they had made use of, for no harm could arise from marking.

The next day, Capt Shortland being offended at the treatment of his friends had received, sent and had three men taken, whom he suspected were concerned in the affair, and put them into the cachot, where they were examined not long after by the King's solicitor, and there ordered to remain till the next Exeter assizes, then and there to be tried by the laws of this country. On the twenty-fifth arrived five hundred suits of clothes, which were distributed among those who had last arrived.

The weather being very severe, and great quantities of snow falling, the men were obliged to keep within doors. On the same day arrived a regiment of regular troops, who themselves had been prisoners in France for many years during the late war between that nation and England.— They were much disgusted with the treatment we received here, and exclaimed against the authors of it, whoever they might be, and declared they had not received such treatment in France.

At this time, the government not being so strict in their charge the military, and the keepers not so strict in putting them in execution, and these new guards being very friendly, gave us a fine opportunity to escape over the walls, and many made their escape in dark stormy nights. This continued for some time, till one man was taken on the wall, in the very act; then it was stopped, and strict orders given.

On the twenty-sixth a draft of prisoners arrived, among whom were the crew of the privateer Neuf-Chattel of New York, lately captured, and two navy officers captured on the lakes. On the twenty-eighth these officers received their parole, and proceeded on to Ashburton, where all the paroled officers were stationed.

### Nantucket Neutrality.

On the thirtieth, Sir Isaac Coffin arrived with another British admiral; Sir Isaac is a native of Massachusetts, and feeling some partiality to his native statesmen, requested Capt. Shortland to permit all the men who belonged to Nantucket to come alone into market square, which request was of course granted. He himself and the other admiral, whose name we did not learn, held a long conversation with the Nantucket men, and inquired the particulars of their birth, their friends and places of residence; they then told them, should the war continue, they would be released, on account of belonging to a neutral Country.—They then took an affectionate leave of the citizens of that neutral nation, and went away. Such are the advantages derived from being a neutral nation in the time of war.

February commences with much snow and cold; the prisoners in great anxiety for the ratification of the treaty.

On the fourth arrived a draft of prisoners, lately captured in the privateer Brutus. At this time a new, and most dreadful calamity now alarmed and endangered the life of every man; the African pox had, by some unfortunate means, got among the prisoners, and threatened destruction to every living soul. The disorder was so violent that when it attacked a person, he had nothing to expect but immediate death; numbers died daily.

On the fifth, the London papers mentioned two American frigates cruising in the channel, which excited great alarm.

On the sixth, the pestilence had grown so mortal, that the chief surgeon in England visited the prison; he imagined the distemper to arise from a want of pure air; that so many people crowded together in one building must render the air very impure, and unfit for respiration. He tried the difference of temperature of the air in the prison, and outside, which he found to differ twenty-five degrees by Farenheit's thermometer, the air being much warmer inside. This difference of heat arose entirely from the heat of the human body, as no fire was kept in the prisons; each prison now contained about 1200 persons on an average. It is highly probable the distemper had generated itself in the bad state of air, and had not been introduced from abroad, as was first supposed.

On the eighth arrived an order from the Board of Transport, for Capt. Shortland to ascertain the number and description of all prisoners belonging to the Island of Nantucket, for the purpose of giving them their discharge; like the citizens of Denmark and Sweden, they were neutral.

On the tenth arrived a draft of prisoners, lately captured on their voyage to France; on the same day a number of prisoners were called on to give evidence on the part of the crown, concerning the marking the traitors in the cheek.

The king's solictor was a long while busy in endeavouring to obtain information, but all the satisfaction he got was, that they had heard by report that the men that marked the traitors, were to be tried at Exeter the next assizes. At the same time a small quantity of clothing arrived from Mr. Beasley, who it seemed always took care to send clothing to those who last arrived, as in this instance, although they had not been prisoners but a few weeks; he seemed to have an idea that they always come into prison naked, and when they were there, one suit would last them all their life; for the oldest prisoners had not received any clothing since the last May, and it was now ten months, and every garment entirely worn out. He supposed, that during two years imprisonment, such as we had had, we must have got used to every species of hardship, and that going naked was so slight an evil that we did not mind it at all.

During the interval of time since the peace, another *slight* evil, somewhat similar to the above, had befallen us, for the contractor, seeing we were shortly to go to a land of plenty, was determined to show us the difference in a man's feelings between eating and going without; so he gave us no more than the simpleton gave his horse while learning him to live without eating.

On the thirteenth, one of the four prisoners, whom we mentioned before were sentenced last August to remain in the cachot during the war, watched an opportunity to get among the other prisoners in the yard, being let into the yard of that building for the benefit of the fresh air, and seeing the attention of the turnkeys and soldiers occupied by some other object, at this time jumped over the iron railing that separated this building from the yards of Nos. 1, 2, and 3, and got undiscovered amongst the other prisoners; the morning following he was missed by the keepers, and information given to Capt. Shortland, who demanded the man from among us immediately that he be returned to the cachot again.

The prisoners positively refused to give the man up, and declared that no force of arms should wrest him from their protection. He then ordered the market closed, and would not allow any communication with it, and refused the prisoners every privilege, and gave them only their allowance.

On the fourteenth, he entered the yard at the head of two hundred soldiers with fixed bayonets, and ordered every prisoner to retire within the prisons, that search might be made for the prisoner, and he again remanded to the cachot; but all the prisoners having previously agreed to stand by each other, and if they attempted to use any violence, to surround and disarm them; a signal was given to surround, and the soldiers were immediately surrounded, and the intention made known to the officers, and advised to retire, unless they were determined to risk the consequence. They then very prudently ordered the soldiers to fall back, and retire without the yard, and leave the man whom they sought.

The captain still harboring rancor in his breast, thought to compel us to give up the man by force of starvation, and kept the markets closed against us, and compelled us to subsist solely on our scant allowance; but we, to retaliate, forbid all prisoners going out of the yard to work, who at this time were about forty or fifty carpenters, masons, and other mechanics, who were a great profit to the government; this step put Shortland to great expense and inconvenience to procure others.

He at last concluded to make peace and restore tranquility, and let the man remain; and, on the twentieth, he again opened the markets to the prisoners, and we permitted the workmen to go out and work again. The other three men remained in the cachot, but a stronger guard was placed? there, otherwise we were determined to release them by force.

On the twenty-second, arrived a draft of prisoners, lately captured off the Cape of Good Hope, among whom were the crew of the late United States brig Syren; the treatment of these men before they arrived at this place will be mentioned in the supplements to this work. These, together with others taken in other parts, arrived since the last enumeration on the last day of one thousand eight hundred and fourteen, made in all at this depot five thousand eight hundred and fifty, which were all the prisoners in England, except officers on parole. The prisoners were barefooted, and very sickly.

On the twenty-sixth of this month, is gazetted in the London papers, the official account of the capture of the United States frigate President, Com. Decatur.

The editor says she was captured solely by the Endymion, of far inferior force; he says the engagement was in the old English style, yard-arm to yard-arm. Knowing this to be a falsehood, I addressed a letter to the editor, requesting him to read a short piece of poetry which I enclosed.

March commenced with cold and blustering weather, and the prison almost one continued scene of sick and dying, the small-pox was raging with a desolating aspect, and the greatest anxiety concerning the ratification of the treaty; afflictions, which seem never to come singly, were now pressing upon the back of one another; pestilence, famine and nakedness were not affliction enough, phrensy must be added.

On the fourth, a man in the hospital, in a sudden fit of insanity, seized a knife and stabbed two of the nurses very dangerously, of which wounds Jonathan Paul died on the tenth, the other survived.

On inquiry into the circumstances of the deceased, we found him to have been a married man, and his wife had lived a little distance from the prison since his confinement, who was in very narrow circumstances.

We all agreed to give her the day's allowance of fish of that week, which we sold to the contractor and received the money, which amounted to nearly one hundred dollars; this sum she received, and returned to her residence on the day of the death of her husband.

On this day, also, the three men who were put into close confinement for marking the traitors on the face, were taken out of the custody of the agent of prisoners of war at this place, by a writ of *habeas corpus ad respodendum*, and removed to the criminal prison at Exeter, to be tried for the offence by the civil laws of this country. They were removed in irons. The prisoners then made a contribution for the support of these men while at Exeter.

On the tenth, we received London papers, which gave an account of Bonaparte's having arrived in France at the head of about one thousand men, and that he was making the most rapid advances toward Paris, and thousands joining him; that the greatest confusion was taking place in the affairs of France.

This intelligence struck the greatest astonishment in all England, and created a very serious concern among all the military, who expected to be relieved on the arrival of the treaty ratified by the President, but now they must despair of that idea, as new wars must inevitably follow the steps of that gigantic monster.

On the fourteenth, a universal joy was diffused through the whole prison, and "a smile lighted up in the aspect of woe;" the Favorite, the welcome messenger of peace, arrived, and brought the treaty, ratified by the President of the United States.

I cannot better express the joy that diffused itself through the whole country, Englishmen as well as prisoners, than by giving the following lines from a great author:

"The dumb shall sing, the lame his crutch forego,

And leap exulting like the bounding roe.

No sigh nor murmur the wide world shall hear,

From ev'ry face he wipes off ev'ry tear."

We raised the ensigns and pendant on each prison; presented to Capt. Shortland, and gentlemen under his command, an address in poetry.

On the seventeenth, we were informed by Capt. Shortland, that he had received orders from the Board of Transport to discharge the prisoners whenever Mr. Beasley was ready to receive them. To the great disappointment of all the prisoners we had received no information from Mr. Beasley for six weeks, and the prisoners now were in the greatest anxiety. They reasonably expected that on the arrival of this ratified treaty, Mr. Beasley would have everything in a state of readiness for their immediate conveyance to the United States, and that he would inform them in what manner they were to proceed there; but not a syllable was received from the agent of our country till the eighteenth, when a very cold and unpleasant letter was received from him, which read as follows:

*Fellow-citizens,—*

I am informed that great numbers of the prisoners refuse being inoculated with the small-pox, which I hear has been very mortal among you, I therefore acquaint you that it will be impossible for me to send home any prisoners unless they have gone through the same. Yours, &c.,

R. G. BEASLEY.

This strange letter rather increased the great anxiety every man was in, for we expected to have been informed something relative to our speedy departure, and that he had made arrangements to clothe the oldest prisoners, who were so naked that they were unfit to be discharged.

On the nineteenth, an order arrived, informing Capt. Shortland to discharge thirty men, as they had been applied for by American captains, to man ships in France and up the east country; the Transport Board had ordered them to be discharged.

On the twentieth, Capt. Shortland released those three men whom we have mentioned were committed to close confinement in the cachot last August, on suspicion of blowing up the vessel; the other, we have mentioned, made his escape.

These men made as ghastly an appearance as it is possible for human beings to make; they had been eight months confined within a damp stone room, twenty feet square, floored with stone, and no light except a dim ray that gleamed through the top of the gable end. They had lived on two-thirds of a scant allowance till their trembling limbs could scarce support their body.

On the same day, a writ came to remove the insane man who had occasioned the death of Jonathan Paul to Exeter, to have his trial; also one to bring forward about twenty persons as witnesses, in this and the trial of the three men whom we mentioned had been taken there for trial for marking the traitors.

The small-pox raged now in a most alarming manner; it being of the African kind, scarce a man recovered after once being attacked and conveyed to the hospital.

After the arrival of the ratification of the treaty, great numbers visited the prison, from all parts of the country, with almost every kind of article for sale in the markets, among whom were great numbers of Jews, who came here to sell old clothes.

One of these Jew merchants, on his way to the prison, met a farmer who lived about eight miles from the prison, and accused him of being an American prisoner, making his escape from the depot, as great numbers had lately made their escape; and, thinking to receive the reward, which was three pounds, given by the government for apprehending any prisoner making his escape from the prison, told the farmer he must go back to the prison with him; and the farmer, having been once a sailor, was willing to confirm him in his suspicions, and began the song of Yankee Doodle; this confirmed the Jew in his belief of his being an American, and he was sure he had got a prize worth three pounds to him; but his prisoner refused to walk, and thinking he could afford to hire a conveyance for him, gave half a guinea to a wagoner to take him to the prison, and treated him very liberally along the way with drink. About 11 o'clock the Jew arrived with his prisoner, and applied to the keepers to take charge of him, and pay the reward of three pounds; but to his astonishment, the clerks, turnkeys, and every officer, immediately knew the farmer, and knew him to be a respectable man residing on the edge of the moor. He now demanded of the Jew a compensation for being detained several hours a prisoner, and the demand being justified by Capt. Shortland, the Jew was obliged to pay five pounds to prevent a suit.

The affair was made known to the prisoners, and every man forbid purchasing anything of the Jew; he was therefore obliged to leave the market without disposing of a single article.

On the twenty-fourth, a letter was received from Mr. Beasley, informing those Americans who had been taken under the French flag, and had been considered French prisoners till they were discharged, and from that time till this, had been recognised by no government, that he was now authorized to acknowledge them as Americans, and sent to each man a suit of clothes. This was the first assistance these men had had from any government since the French prisoners were discharged, and had lived entirely on the charity of the other prisoners. They had been prisoners four or five years.

The same letter informed us that he had taken three ships at London for the conveyance of the prisoners to the United States.

The same day a passport for four prisoners, who were to be discharged, was received.

During this month many prisoners made their escape, the government appearing very careless; and it was supposed this negligence was intentional, that they might escape for the purpose of impressing, as the press was hot about this time; but some few were detected when passing the wall, and sentenced to the cachot for ten days, on two-thirds allowance, which stopped the escaping for that time.

On the twenty-fifth the prisoners began to be impatient of such delay in the American agent, as eleven days had elapsed since the arrival of the ratified treaty, and nothing in readiness to discharge them, no means provided, and such delay too much to be borne; their situation was such that they could not restrain their resentment against such criminal neglect as their agent was guilty of; they were determined to punish him as much as it lay in their power; they therefore caused his effigy to be hanged on the top of one of the prisons, after which it was taken down, and burnt in presence of all the officers and soldiers—But I must not forget to mention the sentence of the court, pronounced before his execution, and his dying confession, when under the gallows.

## Sentence.

At this trial, held at Dartmoor on the twenty-fifth day of March, one thousand eight hundred and fifteen, you, Reuben G. Beasley in effigy, are found guilty, by an impartial and judicious jury of your countrymen, upon the testimony of five thousand seven hundred witnesses, of depriving many hundreds of your countrymen of their lives, by the most wanton and most cruel deaths, by nakedness, starvation, and exposure to pestilence. It therefore becomes the duty of this court, as ought to be the duty of every court of justice, to pronounce that sentence of the law, which your manifold and heinous crimes so richly deserve.—And it is with the deepest regret that I am compelled to say, our country has been imposed upon, by a man whose crimes must cut him off from among the living. You this day must be hanged by the neck on the top of the prison No. 7, until you are dead; your body is then to be taken down and fastened to a stake, and burned to ashes, which are to be distributed to the winds, that your name may be forgotten, and your crimes no longer disgrace our nation.

On hearing the above sentence, the compunction of his conscience now brought forth the following confession:

## CONFESSION.

*Injured countrymen and fellow-citizens:*

I this day, by the verdict of a just and impartial jury, and by the sentence of an impartial court, am to be made a public example, and receive that punishment which is so justly due to my many odious offences against the laws of God and my country; and being in a very few moments to make my exit from this world, do confess, in the presence of Almighty God, that for the first twelve months of my consulship I did most criminally neglect the American prisoners, who were dying daily for the want of my assistance, which I withheld through mercenary motives: the cries and petitions of my unfortunate countrymen I have always treated with the utmost disregard and contempt, but being fully convinced of all my past errors, I make this public and candid confession, in hopes that I may find mercy in the presence of a just and merciful God. I further do acknowledge, that I have been the means of detaining you in your present situation by neglecting to send you home, as I might have done, while the exchange was open for prisoners, which was not closed till June, eighteen hundred and thirteen; I likewise confess, that I have deprived great numbers of you of your regular turns of exchange, by filling the cartels with paroled officers, who were not entitled to the same; I must confess that had I have made proper application to the British government, and had I used my influence, I might have obtained the release of all the men discharged from his majesty's ships of war; but being selfish, and swayed by despicable motives, I made no exertions for their relief. I do likewise confess, that after the second year of my consulship, I could no longer withhold from my unfortunate countrymen, some little assistance in money and clothing, as the United States had given me positive orders to supply all the wants of her citizens, who were prisoners of war at that time in England; but to my shame, and to the disgrace of any American agent, I entered in a contract with a *Jew merchant* of London, to supply the prisoners with the very meanest and coarsest clothing that could possibly be procured in all England. At the same time I made advances to you, prisoners, of two and a half cents per day, and then represented to your country, the Congress of the United States, that I had supplied all your wants by providing you a sufficient quantity of clothing, and making you a daily advance of money suitable to your wants; for I did think that by deceiving the United States, and depriving you of the necessaries of life, I should in a very few years accumulate to myself a very handsome fortune; but to my great disappointment and disgrace, the peace took place, and all my villany and deception was discovered; my crimes stood in open day. For these crimes now I am justly doomed to this ignominious death, and must very shortly make my appearance before the just and Almighty God, to answer for all my crimes; where I expect there will rise up in evidence against me, the souls of hundreds of my departed countrymen, who now lie buried behind the walls of this prison by my crimes; as the time is now expired, I must depart to the uncertainty of an hereafter.

The hat drops.

I depart among the damned.

After the ashes was scattered in the winds, the following dirge was then sung:

The image of disgrace we've hang'd,

And wish it was quite true

That Beasley had himself been there,

And the devil burnt his Jew:

For both contriv'd to wrong us much;

And they know it very well,

They'll always have the prisoners' prayer

To send them both to HELL.

On the twenty-sixth, the prisoners who had been taken to Exeter to give evidence against the insane man who stabbed Paul, and also those who were to give evidence against the three men who were accused of marking the traitors, returned to Dartmoor; as did also the defendants who had had their trial, and were acquitted.

On the twenty-eighth, we received our monthly pay as usual: the prison continued very sickly, and no preparation for our departure.

At this time the officers and soldiers of the garrison seemed greatly alarmed and much concerned at the news received from France. They had the greatest apprehensions of an immediate war with Bonaparte, as the Paris papers gave an account of his being at the head of three hundred thousand men in arms; and the British papers mentioned the great preparations they were making in this country to assist the allies. The very name of the Emperor, and the mention of the battle of New-Orleans, made every British officer and soldier turn pale, and shudder at the thought.

On the last day of March, I collected the exact number of all prisoners at this depot, and noted as follows:

| | |
|---|---|
| In prison No. 1 | 1769 |
| In do. No. 3 | 972 |
| In do. No. 4 | 1051 |
| In do. No. 5 | 958 |
| In do. No. 7 | 1263 |
| In different employments about the stores | 51 |
| Employed in the hospital | 19 |
| Patients in the hospital | 130 |
| Total at Dartmoor | 5693 |

The following are the different descriptions of prisoners, and the number of each class.

| | |
|---|---|
| There were of those discharged from British ships of war, and also those taken in England, | 2200 |
| Colored people | 1000 |
| United States' soldiers and sailors | 250 |
| Taken on board of privateers and merchant-ships, Including those few mentioned, taken under the French flag. | 2243 |

On the same day we received letters from London, informing us that the ships taken for our conveyance, lay wind bound in the Downs.

The month concluded with pleasant weather for Dartmoor; sickness and small pox had somewhat abated.

The prisoners made a contribution for the assistance of a prisoner, who had lost an arm in attempting to take possession of the cartel, which was conveying them from Halifax to England.

As this is intended to be a true and faithful account of all the occurrences and circumstances of the American captives in England, we cannot forbear mentioning some circumstances, which may appear trifling and uninteresting to those who have not felt as we have.

The weather now being mild, and the pleasant season for crossing the Atlantic fast approaching, the prisoners felt the most insufferable anxiety for their departure. The winds being favorable, and seventeen days having elapsed since the ratified treaty arrived, they could not but wait with impatience for the cartels.

On the first of March, Capt. Shortland received orders to discharge twenty-one prisoners, who had applied to be released in England. Previous to this time almost all the men who had been delivered from the British ships of war, had been paid at different times their prize money, and the wages due for their past services in the navy.

This day a man by the name of Bratt, who had belonged to the United States' brig Argus returned to prison. This man, at the time we were attempting to make our escape by digging out, was accused of dropping some unguarded expression, which had led to a discovery of our first attempt; he was threatened to be put to death, by great numbers of prisoners, and the keepers fearing this might be the case, took him to the guard house, where he remained till the crew of the Argus were discharged from prison, when he was also discharged with them, and went along with the crew to Dartmouth, and entered the cartel; he was there accused of the same as before, and threatened, and fearing his life might be taken, he escaped from the cartel, went into the country and worked at his trade, which was that of a blacksmith, and had resided there the whole time.

On the second we had information that the ship Milo, of Boston, had arrived in England in eighteen days from that port; she was the first American vessel which had reached this place since the peace.

On the same day, we received a letter from Mr. Beasley, which read as follows:

*Fellow Citizens,*

From the numberless letters I receive daily, I find that the prisoners entertain an idea of my releasing any prisoners that are enabled with a sufficiency to provide for themselves; I therefore must give you fully my intention on that subject, which is, to grant passports only to such persons as have friends or connexions in this country, of responsibility.

I must also acquaint you that I am making every possible dispatch with the cartels for your conveyance to the United States, where you are much wanted, and the encouragement for seamen very great.

This letter again revived the drooping spirits of the prisoners, who for many days had been almost distracted with the tedium of suspense. We now felt that a few days would release us from this earthly hell, and like Ænas of old, pass by propitious gales from hell to heaven, and shortly repose on the Elysian fields, in the arms of the goddess of liberty.

The prisoners that had kept shops in the prisons for retailing small articles, such as tobacco, thread, soap, coffee, sugar, &c. now broke up, and every thing was in great confusion for want of these articles; these shops were a great advantage to those who kept them, and a great accommodation to all the prisoners. There had been from sixty to eighty in each prison; at these places all these small articles might easily be obtained, though at somewhat higher price than in the market.

Our salary would not go far in purchasing these articles, which were very high at this time all over England; we could buy for a penny sterling, only one small chew of tobacco, which was selling at Plymouth by the quantity at nine shillings and six pence per pound.

We find mentioned in the paper of this day, the arrival of the late U. States frigate President at Plymouth; they barely mention that she had arrived at that place, and that she was captured by the Endymion, but the circumstances of the capture they very prudently left out, as reflecting no honor on the captors.

Capt. Shortland had two men committed to close confinement, who had been accused of drawing money from the Directors of Greenwich Hospital, under assumed names.

On the fourth, a circumstance occurred, which may lead to the recital of other circumstances, which many to whose hand this work may come, may be inclined to doubt the veracity of; but I can appeal, not only to those who have certified this work, but to nearly six thousand of my fellow prisoners, who upon their solemn oath can attest to the truth of what is herein contained.

During the whole of this day the prisoners remained without bread, and the captain of the prison gone to Plymouth: we were obliged to subsist on the four and a half ounces of beef, and the soup made of it; we demanded of the contractor the reason of our not drawing our usual allowance of bread; he answered, that it could not be obtained till to-morrow; we waited as patiently as our feelings would allow, till the expiration of thirty-six hours from the time we had received the last bread, when hunger became so pressing, that it drove us to a state of desperation, and we could no longer endure it, as the whole allowance was scarcely sufficient to sustain life. At dusk in the evening, we again demanded the reason of our not receiving our allowance of bread as usual, as the store-house we well knew contained a sufficiency of both hard and soft bread. The contractor's clerk informed us, that a quantity of damaged hard bread, which had been kept in reserve for times of extreme necessity, now remained on hand, and that unless we would accept of one pound of that in lieu of the pound and a half of soft bread allowed by the Transport Board, until all they had was expended, he should not serve us with any bread, until Capt. Shortland returned from Plymouth.

The prisoners then collected themselves into companies, to consider of this very extraordinary conduct in the contractor; and after mature deliberation, they all concluded that it must be a design in the contractor to get rid of his damaged bread, before we went away, and had taken this opportunity, while the captain was absent, to compel us to receive it by starving us till we were willing; we therefore concluded rather to die by the sword, than the famine, and determined to remain no longer in this starving condition, for we had all this time lived solely on the four and a half ounces of beef. Thus desperate by starvation, we determined to force open the gates in front of the prison, disarm the soldiers, break open the store-house and supply ourselves; and provided the garrison should charge or fire upon us, to make a general attack, and take possession of the guard house and barracks, and stand the consequences let come what might. Accordingly at dark, the prisoners were ordered, as usual, inside the prisons to be locked up for the night, but instead of complying with orders, a signal previously agreed on was given, and passed like lightning through every prison, and every prisoner appeared instantly at the gate in one solid body; on approaching the gates, and bursting open the first three, the soldiers and turnkeys stationed there, fled in the utmost confusion and consternation to the main body in the guard house. The alarm-bells rung and the drums in every direction around the garrison beat to arms; the women in the different houses connected to the depot, flew in confusion and terror in every direction from the depot; in a few moments the alarm had reached the neighboring villages for many miles, and the militia assembled in arms to assist the garrison, which was at this time twelve hundred. We stood arranged in front of the store-house ready to receive the attack of the soldiery, or receive our usual allowance of bread; in a few moments the soldiers arrived and advanced with charged bayonets within two yards of the prisoners. The soldiers were then brought to a stand by the threats of the prisoners who all declared, in the most determined tone, that if they attempted to fire or make a charge on them, they must abide by any consequences that would follow: we told them that we were confident that no such orders had been issued by the government of Great Britain; we also told them, that unless the bread was served out immediately, that the store-house should be levelled with the ground, and every prisoner should march out of the prison. The contractor, clerks, &c. then immediately came forward and entered into this engagement, that if the prisoners would retire into the prison yards, that the bread should be immediately served to them; the prisoners agreed and retired, and for the securing the fulfilment of the engagement, they took with them as a hostage one of the clerks inside of the prison, and there to remain till every prisoner had received his usual allowance of bread, which was not till after twelve o'clock at night. During this time, the guards, soldiers, keepers, and every person connected with the prison, remained in the greatest apprehension, fearing the prisoners had some further intention than merely to obtain their bread; they feared their troubles would end in a more serious way, and the prisoners all make their escape. But next morning showed that the prisoners had no intention of escaping, for during the confusion of the night, many of them had taken the opportunity to scale the walls in an opposite direction, while the attention of the guard was taken up with the main body of them.

Those that had gone out after remaining all night, came and demanded admittance into prison again. This movement in the prisoners astonished the natives of the moor, who left vacant their huts and fled for safety; and the women and children had retired to the nearest towns, and there took refuge, and the men had joined the garrison for protection.

During the night an express was sent to Plymouth to acquaint Capt. Shortland of the event, and that the prisoners had complete possession of the whole garrison, and the control of all things at Dartmoor. In the morning Capt. Shortland arrived with a reinforcement of two hundred soldiers; but found all things quiet and tranquil; as the prisoners had obtained their usual allowance of bread, they were satisfied and sought nothing more. Capt. Shortland made an apology for the conduct of the contractor, and things passed on tolerably well; but great suspicions remained among the people who had formerly attended the market, and these had spread abroad and become the general opinion outside the walls, that the American prisoners being detained so long since the ratification had arrived, now three weeks, in which time Mr. Beasley might have had all discharged and on their passage to the United States, had grown impatient; and as no ships had yet sailed from London to receive them, their forbearance was quite exhausted, and from some threats that had been thrown out by some of the prisoners in presence of the market people, that if the agent of their country did not procure their release within one month from the arrival of the treaty, that they would take their liberty in a body, being determined to risk their lives at all hazards, and depend on their own exertions for their liberty among armed soldiers, rather than remain in the wretched condition they were then in. These suspicions had gone so much abroad, that every body about the prison was apprehensive the prisoners would make the attempt to escape in a body, and some unhappy issue grow out of it. But the prisoners generally had no design of escaping, as by that means they would lose their opportunity of returning home in the cartels. On the sixth, we addressed a letter to Mr. Beasley, on the subject of our discharge, and informed him that we had made application to the British Government to interfere in forwarding our release, as he, Mr. Beasley, had delayed the time already nearly one month, and had only procured three ships, and them still in London, when at the same time ships could have been procured at Plymouth, on equally as good terms as at London, which would, with very little exertion on the part of Mr. Beasley, have released the greater part of the prisoners in two weeks from the arrival of the ratification of the treaty.

The story I am about to relate is of the deepest concern, as well to every citizen of the United States as to those who were the immediate subjects of it. The event concerns the interest of both governments, and deserve to be treated in the most candid and impartial manner; every transaction whereby the intention of those acting in it can be discovered, require to be shown in the purest and most open view.

That the public may have all that can be known on this important subject, I purpose to lay before them, in the first instance, what passed within my own knowledge, that I myself was witness to; then to give them the report of the committee appointed by the prisoners to investigate the circumstances of the massacre; and lastly, to give the report of the agents appointed by the two governments.

What one of that Nation, or what soldier of that hardened, wretched band, can refrain from tears even while he relates the murderous deeds?

"What blind, detested madness could afford,

Such horrid license to the murd'ring sword!"

Though the scene is of painful memory, and my soul shudders at the remembrance, and hath shrunk back with grief at the thought, yet will I relate what my eyes hath seen and my ears heard.

On the sixth of this month, April, about six o'clock in the evening, Capt. Shortland discovered a hole in the inner wall, that separates the barrack-yard from prison No. 6 and 7; this hole had been made in the afternoon by some prisoners out of mere play, without any design to escape.

On discovering the hole, Capt. Shortland seemed instantly to conceive the murderous design; for, without giving the prisoners any notice to retire, he planted soldiers in proper positions on the top of the wall, where they could best assist in perpetrating his murderous and barbarous deeds.

A few minutes past six, while the prisoners were innocently, and unapprehensive of danger, walking in the prison yards and those in No. 1, 3 and 4 were particularly so, as the yards of these prisons are entirely separated every way from the yard in which the hole in the wall had been made—the alarm bells rung, and the drums of the garrison in every direction beat to arms; this was about ten minutes past six.

This sudden and unexpected alarm excited the attention of all the prisoners, who, out of curiosity made immediately for the prison yard to inquire the reason of the alarm.

Among so many as were in this depot, it is reasonable to suppose that some mischievous persons were among them, and among those collected at the gate were some such persons who forced the gate open, whether by accident or design I will not attempt to say; but without any intention of making an escape, and totally unknown to every man, except the few who stood in front of the gates; those back naturally crowded forward to see what was going on at the gates; this pressed and forced a number through the gates, quite contrary to the intention of either those in front or those in rear.

While in this situation Capt. Shortland entered the inner square, at the head of the whole body of soldiers in the garrison; as soon as they entered, Capt.

Shortland took sole command of the whole, and immediately drew up the soldiers in a position to charge.

The soldier-officers, perceiving by this move the horrid and murderous design of Capt. Shortland, resigned their authority over the soldiers, and refused to take any part, or give any orders for the troop to fire.

They saw by this time that the terrified prisoners were retiring as fast as so great a crowd would permit, and hurrying and flying in terrible flight, in every direction, to their respective prisons.

The troop had now advanced within three yards of the prisoners, when Capt. Shortland gave them orders to charge upon them; at this time the prisoners had all got within their respective prison yards, and were flying with the greatest precipitation from the point of the bayonet; the doors now being full of the terrified crowd, they could not enter as fast as they wished; at this moment of dismay, Capt. Shortland was distinctly heard to give orders to the troops to fire upon the prisoners, although now completely in his power, and their lives at his disposal, and had offered no violence, nor attempted to resist, and the gates all closed.

The order was immediately obeyed by his soldiers, and they discharged a full volley of musketry into the main body of the prisoners, on the other side of the iron railings which separated the prisoners from the soldiers.

These volleys were repeated for several rounds, and the prisoners falling, either dead or wounded, in all directions, while it was yet impossible for them to enter the prison, on account of the numbers that flew there for refuge from the rage of the blood thirsty murderer.

In the midst of this horrid slaughter, one man among the rear prisoners, with great presence of mind and the most undaunted courage, turned and advanced to the soldiers, amidst the fire of hundreds, and while his fellow-prisoners were falling all around him, and in an humble and suppliant manner, with his hat in his hand, this resolute soul, in the face of danger and death, implored mercy of Capt. Shortland to spare his countrymen. "O! spare my countrymen!" he cried, "O! Captain, forbear, don't kill us all." To this supplication, this cruel, inexorable Shortland replied, "Retire, you dammed rascal; I'll hear to nothing." The soldiers then pricked him with their bayonets, which compelled him to retreat to the prison door, where he must wait his doom with the other unfortunate prisoners, till the soldiers, who had now entered the different prison yards, and were pursuing and firing should dispatch him with the rest.

To do justice to the merits of this young man, I must inform the public that his name is Greenlow, of Virginia, and late a midshipman in the United

States navy, but now a prisoner of the crew of the privateer Prince of Neufchattel.

The soldiers now advanced, making a general massacre of men and boys, whom accident or impossibility had left without the doors of the prison; they advanced near to the crowded doors, and instantly discharged another volley of musketry on the backs of those farthest out, endeavoring to force their passage into the prison.

This barbarous act was repeated in the presence of this inhuman monster, Shortland—and the prisoners fell, either dead or severely wounded, in all directions, before his savage sight.

But his vengeance was not glutted by the cruel murder of the innocent men and boys that lay weltering and bleeding in the groans and agonies of death along the prison-doors, but turned and traversed the yard, and hunted a poor affrighted wretch, that had flew for safety close under the walls of prison No. 1, and dared not move lest he should be discovered, and immediate death be his lot.

But, alas! the unhappy man was discovered by these hell-hounds, with this demon at their head, and with cool and deliberate malice, drew up their muskets to their shoulders and despatched the unhappy victim, while in the act of imploring mercy from their hands. His only crime was not being able to get into the prison without being shot before.

In the yard of No. 7, they found in their hunt another hapless victim, crouching close along the wall at the far end of the yard, and fearing to breathe, lest he should share the fate of his unfortunate countrymen that had already fallen a sacrifice to the rage of this lawless banditti; when, O! cruel to relate, five of them drew up the instruments of death, and by the order of this fell murderer, discharged their contents into the body of this innocent man, while begging them to spare his life!

This *Nero*, now having accomplished his murderous designs, retired with his troops from the yard, and left it a horrid scene of his relentless rage!

The dead and the wounded lay scattered about the yard; seven were killed dead on the spot, and six with the loss of a leg or an arm, and dangerously wounded; several were pronounced mortal. The names of every man, either killed or wounded will be given in the catalogue annexed.

As it was much feared the murderers would endeavor to conceal many of the dead, Dr. Magrath, head surgeon of the Hospital, an honest skillful man, entered immediately after Shortland retired, and exerted his utmost ability in collecting the dead and wounded from the several prison yards, and conveying them to the Hospital.

At the same time he sent to the neighboring towns to call in the aid of medical gentlemen that resided there; he also demanded admittance into the prisons, which were now closed, to receive the dead and wounded that had reached the inside of the prison.

A despatch was immediately sent to Plymouth, to inform the Admiral and Commodore, and the Commander in Chief of the Military Department, of the fatal *sixth of April, one thousand eight hundred and fifteen*; which day must be of horrid memory to every American, whose mind will revolt with indignity at the name of SHORTLAND AND THE MASSACRE AT DARTMOOR!!

*Shortland!* thou foul monster and inhuman villain! is thy soul glutted with the blood of the innocent victims, that Fate had doomed to thy revengeful and blood-thirsty power? I appeal to the world to say whether the conduct of Warren Hastings, whether the massacre of St. Domingo, can exceed the horrid catastrophe of this ill-fated night, conducted under the immediate inspection of your murderous eye? and should the laws of your country not doom you to a death of the most severe nature as a public example for your well known crimes? Your whole nation is involved as a black accomplice in your monstrous guilt; and the blood of my unfortunate countrymen, shed by your base hand, must ever remain a stain to the character of your nation.

Tell me, *ye* bloody butchers! and *thou* who contrived, as well as ye who executed the execrable design, how dare ye breathe that air, which wafted to the ear of Majesty the groans of the wounded and the dying? How dare ye tread that earth which is wet with the blood of the innocent, shed by your accursed hands? Do not the goads and stings of conscious guilt wound you in your daily walks? Do not the ghosts of the murdered rise before you in your nightly dreams?

On the morning of the seventh, by order of the commander-in-chief at Plymouth, a Colonel, with a reinforcement of troops, arrived and took command of the depot. Immediately on his arrival, he sent notice to the prisoners of his taking the command, and that Capt. Shortland wished the prisoners to appoint some few men to receive the explanation of his last night's conduct; but we unanimously agreed, and despatched a letter to the Colonel, acquainting him that as citizens of the United States of America, we should conceive it a disgrace to the national character of our country to hold any communication with the murderer of our fellow-citizens. But provided the Colonel should require any conference with the prisoners, they should at any time with pleasure attend, and explain the nature of every past event.

The Colonel, requesting a conference, came to the gate attended by the guilty Shortland, who could not now disguise the guilt of his crime; he could not look a prisoner in the face; as he walked along towards the prison bars with his eyes fixed on the ground, and as he came to the spot where, a few hours before, lay one of our murdered countrymen, he saw the blood, and faintly attempted to speak; but the monitor of Heaven was not quite overcome by the powers of Hell, and he could not utter a word. After several efforts he hesitatingly attempted to justify his conduct by saying it was a part of his duty, which was grounded on the fear he had of the prisoners making an attempt to escape, and imputed part of the fault to Mr. Beasley, in driving the prisoners to a state of desperation by his great delay of sending them home.

The Colonel very patiently heard the stories of both parties, and promised a jury of inquest should be held over the bodies of our departed countrymen the next day, and a strict investigation of every circumstance of the event had, according to evidence.

At nine o'clock we hoisted the colors half-mast on every prison; we then visited the Hospital, but the spectacle was painful indeed, and enough to freeze the blood of the most hardened parricide; the tables were covered with the amputated legs and arms of our fellow-prisoners, and our ears stunned with the groans of forty-two, wounded in the most shocking manner; and seven lay dead as solemn witnesses of the horrid act.

We then returned to the prisons and appointed a committee of ten to take depositions of a great number of persons who were best acquainted with the particular facts. The committee being severally sworn, proceeded to make all possible inquiry into the circumstances of the massacre, and prepare every testimony to lay before the jury which were to sit over the bodies the next day.

At two in the afternoon arrived an Admiral and another officer of high rank in his Majesty's navy, and after introducing themselves to the prisoners, in a very friendly and feeling manner, expressed their extreme regret for the horrid and barbarous act of Capt. Shortland, and informed us that they had come clothed with proper authority to make inquiry into the conduct of Capt. Shortland in the late unhappy event and his conduct during his agency at the prison. They assured us, that he would be called to an account by the government, and that a fair investigation should be had of all his conduct.

I have omitted to mention a circumstance which occurred during the dreadful scene of the night. A lamp-lighter, who was in the act of lighting the lamp at the door of prison No. 3, in which I myself resided, being compelled to take refuge among the prisoners, was forced by the hurrying group into the prison. He belonged to the same regiment of soldiers who were that moment committing these most horrid outrages. He was immediately seized by the prisoners, and conveyed to a particular part of the prison, and the prisoners being in the most enraged state, it was immediately proposed to put him to death, and sacrifice him to our resentment, as a just retaliation of our injury; but on cool deliberation and debate throughout the prison, it was thought better to spare him; and to the pleasing astonishment of this man, half dead with fear, he was told to rest easy, for his life should not be taken, but he should be preserved, that the whole world might distinguish the difference of humanity between unprovoked British soldiers, and the injured and provoked American seamen; accordingly, when the doors were opened to take out the wounded, the man was released, which astonished and confounded the whole soldiery, who felt the force of the reproach with the keenest remorse, and were compelled to express the highest respect for this generous revenge.

*The following is a correct list of killed and wounded on the 6th of April, 1815, and contains a true statement of their condition at 12 o'clock on the 8th day of the same month.*

## KILLED.

John Haywood, black, Virginia, discharged; the ball entered a little posterior to the acromion of the left shoulder, and passed obliquely upwards; made about the middle of the right side its egress of the neck.

Thomas Jackson, N. Y. Orbit of N. Y., the ball entered the left side of the belly nearly in a line with the navel, and made its egress a little below the false ribs in the opposite side; a large portion of the intestinal canal protruded through the wound made by the ingress of the ball. He languished until 3 o'clock of the 7th, when he died.

John Washington, Maryland, Rolla privateer; the ball entered at the squamore process of the left temporal bone, and passing through the head, made its exit a little below the cruceal ridge of the occipital bone.

James Mann, Boston, Ciro; the ball entered at the inferior angle of the left scapula, and lodged under the integument of the right pectoral muscle. In its course, it passed through the inferior margin of the right and left lobes of the lungs.

Joseph Toker Johnson, not known; the ball entered at the inferior angle of the left scapula, penetrated the heart, and passing through both lobes of the lungs, made its egress at the right axilla.

William Leverage, N. Y., Saratoga; the ball entered about the middle of the left arm, through which it passed, and penetrating the corresponding side, betwixt the second and third ribs, passing through the left lobe of the lungs, the mediartenum, and over the right lobe, lodged betwixt the fifth and sixth ribs.

James Campbell, N. Y., discharged; the ball entered at the outer angle of the right eye, and in its course fractured and depressed the greater part of the frontal bone, fractured the nasal bones, and made its egress above the orbital ridge of the left eye. He languished until the morning of the 8th, when he died.

### DANGEROUSLY WOUNDED, AND LIMBS AMPUTATED IMMEDIATELY ON THE NIGHT OF THE SIXTH.

John Gray, Virginia, prize to the Paul Jones, left arm.
James Wills, Marblehead, Paul Jones, left arm.
James Trumbull, Portland, Maine, Elbridge Gerry, left arm.
Robbert Willett, Portland, Maine, left thigh.
Thomas Smith, New-York, Paul Jones, left thigh.
John Gier, Boston, Rambler, left thigh.
Wm. Leversage, N. Y., Magdalen, right thumb.

### DANGEROUSLY WOUNDED, LIMBS NOT AMPUTATED ON THE EIGHTH.

Thomas Findley, Marblehead, Enterprise, wounded in the thigh and back.

Ephraim Linson.

John Hogerberth, Philadelphia, Good Friends, of do., thigh and hip.

William Blake, Kennebeck, discharged, M. W., three wounds in the body.

Peter Wilson, New-York, Virginia Planter, in the hand.

James Israel, do., do., thigh.

Jacob Davis, do., do., thigh.

Caleb Cotton, Taunton, Mass., M. W., two places in the body.

John Roberts, do., do., thigh.

Joseph Phipps, Old Concord, Zebra, thigh and belly.

William Lamb, do., do., eyes.

Edward Gardner, Marblehead, impressed, in the wrist.

William Appleby, New-York, Magdelen, arm.

James Bell, Philadelphia, Joel Barlow, wrist and thigh.

Philip Ford, Philadelphia, impressed, five wounds, side, breast, back and thigh.

James Birch, thigh.

Henry Montcalm, Roxbury, Mass., Governor Tompkins, knee.

Andrew Garrison, thigh and head.

Robert Tadley, Bath, Maine, Grand Turk, privates.

William Penn, Virginia, impressed, thigh.

Joseph Reugh, thigh.

Thaddeus Howard, Rochester, Mass., Hart of Bedford, leg.

Edward Banker, Portsmouth, N. H., impressed, back.

Thomas George, Norfolk, Virginia, U. S. Rattlesnake, thigh.

Alexander Wilson, Providence, R. I., Leo, hand and leg.

John Surrey, N. Y., French privateer, cheek.

Nathaniel Wakeneld, Beverly, Mass., Ciro, right knee.

Samuel E. Tyler, Boston, Tom, thigh and arm.

Joseph Reaver, Salem, Mass., legs and thighs.

Stephen S. Vincent, New-Jersey, head and ears.

James Christie, Tickler, different places.

William Smith, New-York.

Robert Willet, Portland, man-of-war, knee.

### SLIGHTLY WOUNDED.

Ephraim Lincoln, Boston, Argus, by the bayonet.
Greenlow, Virginia, different places.
James Newman, Baltimore, impressed, by the bayonet.
Alexander Peterson, New-York, Erin, Boston, by the bayonet.
Joseph Music, Charleston, S. C., impressed, by the bayonet.
John Willet, Philadelphia, by the bayonet.
Joseph Hindil, Philadelphia, Young Wasp, in the hand.
Perry Richardson, Bath, Maine, Rolla, by the bayonet.
John Cowen, Teezer, by the bayonet.
James Barker, Wiscasset, Elbridge Gerry, by the bayonet.
James Wedgewood, Portsmouth, N. H., Lark, in the head.
James Mathews, Delaware, by the bayonet.

John Murray, New-York, by the bayonet.
William Marshal, Lawrence, by the bayonet.
Thomas Johnson, Albany, Criterion, by the bayonet.

The list of killed and wounded contains all that could be ascertained at that time, but great suspicions remained among the prisoners that more had been killed than were certainly known, as some were missing, and not to be found among the living or the dead; it was supposed that these had been killed, and being mangled in a most shocking manner, were privately taken away by Capt. Shortland, and buried that night, before Doctor Magrath entered the yard, and a report prevailed that he had done it: as great numbers who were slightly wounded did not go to the hospital, I, to ascertain the exact number of killed and wounded, took the list of those in the hospital, from the doctor's books, and every prison mustered all those that refused going to the hospital, by which means the list can be depended on as strictly correct.

At twelve o'clock, at noon, on the eighth, a jury of inquest arrived, composed of twelve farmers, and a coroner, and sat over the bodies of our murdered countrymen; they began to take the depositions of the prisoners and turnkeys, and proceeded on till seven in the evening, and adjourned till next morning.

The evidence of the prisoners corresponded with the statement in a preceding page.

On the morning of the ninth, the dead not yet being buried, the jury sat over them again, and proceeded on with the evidence on both sides, which consisted of Dr. Magrath, whose evidence was against Shortland, prisoners, turnkeys, soldier-officers, soldiers, &c.

The summary of the evidence I shall give presently; but I must here digress a little to give some circumstances that intervened betwixt the taking of the depositions, and the verdict of the jury.

This morning an order arrived for the discharge of thirty-four prisoners, who had applied to be released to man ships in different parts of Europe.

During the eighth and ninth, the prisoners made every inquiry in their power to learn whether any were missing, who were not included among the dead, wounded, or discharged; but nothing satisfactory could be obtained, but only a report that after the prisons were closed, Capt. Shortland had secretly buried some of the most mangled bodies, before Dr. Magrath entered, as he is a man of integrity, feeling, candor, firmness, and unshaken veracity, as well as genius and skill, that no favor or affection could swerve from the truth. Shortland would therefore endeavor to conceal as much as possible from him, as whatever came within his knowledge, came out without fear or reward, and was much against the conduct of Capt. Shortland. On the morning of the seventh, as before mentioned, we ascertained by the testimony of those persons whose names are mentioned in the certificate to this work, the particulars of the killed and wounded, whose names have been already mentioned, the number of which and their situation, were as follows:

Seven were killed dead in the yards, and in the prisons. Six suffered amputation of a leg or an arm. *Thirty-eight* dangerously wounded and many supposed to be mortal by the surgeon of the depot. *Twelve* slightly wounded. The total amount of killed and wounded *sixty-three*. Among these were many mangled in the most horrid manner, having received five, six, and seven wounds apiece from the bayonet. Hundreds of the prisoners very narrowly escaped, having received several shots through the hats and clothes.

We have just discovered that the soldiers here at present are the Somersetshire militia; and the garrison consists of fifteen hundred soldiers of different military classes.

On the evening of the ninth, the inquest, consisting of twelve peasants, dependants of Capt. Shortland, delivered in this most extraordinary and unjust verdict, of Justifiable Homicide; such a verdict astonished every person, who was not *particeps criminis*. This verdict seems to have been given against evidence; a summary of which on both sides I shall now proceed to give the reader, that he may judge for himself. It appeared from the different witnesses before mentioned, that the hole made in the wall was unknown to more than three-fourths of the prisoners confined in the yard of No. 5 and 7, where the hole was made, and that no combination had ever been entered into by any of the prisoners to escape; it was also proved that the prisoners confined in the yards of No. 1, 3 & 4, were totally ignorant of there being any hole in the wall. It was proved that the gates were broken open by a man in the state of intoxication, and unknown to the prisoners, and that when broken open it was in the power of the sentry to have taken the offender and confined him without any resistance of the prisoners. It was also proved that they came running to the gate out of curiosity, to learn the occasion of the alarm bells ringing; that the few persons (who were not above fifty,) flocked into the square, were carried out of the gates by the numbers pressing in the rear to gratify their curiosity; that no stones or clubs were thrown while they were in this situation; that they all immediately retired into the yards of their respective prisons, and shut the gates after them; that Capt. Shortland took the immediate command of the soldiers, and ordered them to fire on the prisoners; that on firing the prisoners made all possible exertion to gain the inside of the prison; but some fell before they could reach it; that the soldiers pursued and fired into the prisons and killed two within the prison; that the soldiers on the ramparts singled out the prisoners, and fired and killed them, as they were going into the prisons; that after all the prisoners had got in, except some few, being frightened, and not able to get into the prisons, ran for refuge close to the walls, and were fired upon singly, and either killed or wounded by several soldiers firing at one. That an officer of low rank assisted under the command of Capt. Shortland, in killing a boy, not over thirteen years old! that a prisoner applied to Capt. Shortland to forbear, and stop the horrid massacre, as the prisoners were retiring as fast as possible, and that Capt. Shortland answered, "retire, you damned rascal, I'll hear to nothing." It was proved that the turnkeys, contrary to the invariable custom, had been in and locked all the doors of each prison, except one; there being four doors to each prison, they had ever before been left open, till a horn was sounded, and the turnkeys cried "turn in, turn in;" but that night no horn was sounded, nor was there any cry to turn in, but the doors secretly locked, which much surprised the few that happened to see the doors locked, but did not suspect any mischief was about to be done; that this was done some time before the usual hour for turning in. Also, that Capt. Shortland actually took hold of a musket with his own hands in conjunction with a soldier, and fired the first gun. That the soldier-officers were unwilling to give any orders to the soldiers, or take any active part in the proceedings.

From the summary of the evidence above given, on the part of the prisoners, it must appear evident to every impartial reader, that Capt. Shortland made the attack with malice prepense. But to give the public the fairest opportunity to judge, I shall give a summary of the evidence on the part of Capt. Shortland, which came all from the mouth of witnesses *particeps criminis*, and acting with him. Those consisted of clerks, turnkeys, and soldiers, who had been the very instruments of the massacre. They deposed and said, that the prisoners were in a state of mutiny, and that great numbers had threatened to escape by forcing through the walls, and that the hole in the wall was big enough for a man to pass through; that the lock on the gate was broken by some prisoner, and that stones were thrown while the prisoners were at the gate, and also clubs and pieces of iron thrown at the guards by the prisoners while there; that great numbers had got into the square, and that they did mean to make their escape. Nothing material could be further drawn from these witnesses.

In the evening of this day, the bodies of our murdered countrymen were buried behind the prison walls in the same manner as before the peace, without form or ceremony, and no prisoner permitted to attend to see the last sad office, which one friend can perform for another in giving the grave its due. O! Britannia, thy boast is gone, thy pride is lost; humanity is fled from thy degenerate sons, and a safer asylum in the bosom of the savage tribes is found. Deny the dead their sacred due!

Thou ingrate race, is this the reward due to men who have labored many years thy faithful servant, and now, after having dragged out a painful imprisonment for two years, and the moment the hope of returning had rekindled the sparks of life, must be massacred in a most barbarous manner, and denied the right of the grave?

I must here relate one instance which occurred a few years ago, and which goes very far to show the inhumanity of those who have had the command of this depot heretofore. In a manuscript which was left here by the French prisoners, which I was this evening perusing, I find the following remarkable circumstance of cruelty related, which took place during their confinement.

Captain Cotgrave being agent, and Dr. Decker head surgeon of the hospital, in December, one thousand eight hundred and nine, a most malignant and contagious disease, bearing the most frightful and mortal symptoms, broke out among the French prisoners, which, in the short space of one month, carried off more than eight hundred.

This unfeeling man, Dr. Decker, caused the coffins to be brought into the rooms of the hospital to receive the bodies: where they often remained several days in readiness to receive the unhappy man fast approaching the end of all his sufferings.

It is said in the manuscript, that this worse than barbarian, would gaze with the greatest satisfaction on the surrounding victims, that he might discover from the very inmost recesses of the heart, what effect the appearance of these coffins had on their exhausted spirits.

However unfeeling this might be, yet their lot was envied by hundreds of their countrymen, who were left to perish in the prison without any assistance, without a friend, and in want of everything; and would not be received into the Hospital by this unfeeling man.

Their extreme sufferings would have moved the heart even of a cannibal, and it is a solitary instance of cruelty, that any one belonging to a civilized nation could rejoice at such a mournful spectacle, and exult over their fellow-beings in the agonies of death, as did this man often, in saying the more deaths the fewer enemies.

Another circumstance is related in the same manuscript, in which Capt. Isaac Cotgrave was the principal actor.

On the eighth of October, one thousand eight hundred and nine, the turnkeys, by mistake, had left one of the prison doors unlocked, which being discovered by some of the prisoners, they determined, if possible, to effect an escape; they got into the yard but, unfortunately, were discovered the very moment they came out, by one of the sentries, who gave the alarm, and instantly a volley of sixty muskets was discharged at them; numbers were wounded, but none killed; they then hastily retired into the prison.

Capt. Cotgrave, the agent, then entered the yard at the head of a large body of troops, and after searching the yard in every direction, and discovering nobody he was retiring, when they discovered a man creeping along the wall; the blood-thirsty monsters instantly fell upon the unhappy victim, and would neither listen to his cries nor prayers, but before he could make himself known to them, several musket-balls had pierced his vital parts, and laid him lifeless on the ground; but they were not content with this; they ran up to him, and ran over and over his lifeless corpse, stabbing it with their bayonets in many places; after having satiated their ferocity, on inspecting the body, they found it to be one of their own men, whom the darkness of the night had prevented them from distinguishing.

In memory of this horrid act, the French prisoners raised a monument on the very spot where it was committed; but the keepers of the prison had it destroyed the same day, for it was a monument of their cruelty.

## THE REPORT OF THE COMMITTEE OF PRISONERS.

We, the undersigned, being each severally sworn on the holy evangelists of the Almighty God, for the investigation of the circumstances attending the late horrid massacre, and having heard the depositions of a great number of witnesses, from our own personal knowledge, and from the depositions given in as aforesaid,

### REPORT AS FOLLOWS:

That on the 6th of April, about six o'clock in the evening, when the prisoners were all quiet in their respective yards, it being about the usual time of turning in for the night, and the greater part of the prisoners being then in the prisons, the alarm bell was rung, and many of the prisoners ran up to the Market-square to learn the occasion of the alarm. There were then drawn up in the Square several hundred soldiers, with Captain Shortland [the Agent] at their head; it was likewise observed, at the same time, that additional numbers of soldiers were posting themselves on the walls round the prison yards. One of them observed to the prisoners, that they had better go into the prisons, for they would be charged upon directly. This, of course, occasioned considerable alarm among them. In this moment of uncertainty, they were running in different directions, inquiring the cause of the alarm—some toward their respective prisons, and some toward the Market-square. When about one hundred were collected in the Square, Captain Shortland ordered the soldiers to charge upon them, which order the soldiers were reluctant in obeying, as the prisoners were using no violence; but on the order being repeated, they made a charge, and the prisoners retreated out of the Square into the prison-yards, and shut the gates after them. Captain Shortland himself opened the gates, and ordered the soldiers to fire in among the prisoners, who were all retreating in different directions toward their respective prisons. It appears there was some hesitation in the minds of the officers, whether or not it was proper to fire upon the prisoners in that situation; on which Shortland seized a musket out of the hands of a soldier, which he fired. Immediately after, the fire became general, and many of the prisoners were either killed or wounded. The remainder were endeavoring to get into the prisons, when going towards the lower doors, the soldiers on the walls commenced firing on them from that quarter, which killed some and wounded others. After much difficulty, [all the doors being closed in the entrance, but one in each prison] the survivors succeeded in gaining the prisons; immediately after which, parties of soldiers came to the doors of Nos. 3 and 4 prisons, and fired several vollies into them through the windows and doors, which killed one man in each prison, and severely wounded others.

It likewise appears, that the preceding butchery was followed up with a disposition of peculiar inveteracy and barbarity.

One man, who was severely wounded in No. 7 prison-yard, and being unable to make his way to the prison, was come up with by the soldiers, whom he implored for mercy, but in vain; five of the hardened wretches immediately levelled their pieces at him, and shot him dead on the spot.— The soldiers who were posted on the walls, manifested equal cruelty, by keeping up a constant fire on every prisoner they could see in the yards endeavoring to get into the prison, when their numbers were very few, and when not the least shadow of resistance could be made or expected. Several of them had got into No. 6 prison cook-house, which was pointed out by the soldiers on the walls, to those who were marching in from the Square; they immediately went up and fired into the same, which wounded several; one of the prisoners ran out with the intention of gaining his prison, but was killed before he reached the door.

On an impartial consideration of the circumstances of the case, we are induced to believe that it was a premeditated scheme in the mind of Captain Shortland, for reasons which we will now proceed to give—as an illucidation of its origin, we will recur back to an event which happened some days previous. Captain Shortland was, at the time, absent at Plymouth, but before going, he ordered the contractor or his clerk to serve out one pound of indifferent hard bread, instead of one pound and a half of soft bread, their usual allowance—this the prisoners refused to receive—they waited all day in expectation of their usual allowance being served out; but at senset, finding this would not be the case, burst open the lower gates, and went up to the store, demanding to have their bread.

The officers of the garrison, on being alarmed, and informed of their proceedings, observed, that it was no more than right the prisoners should have their usual allowance, and strongly reprobated the conduct of Captain Shortland in withholding it from them. They were accordingly served with their bread, and quietly returned to their prison. This circumstance, with the censures that were thrown on his conduct, reached the ears of Shortland on his return home, and he must then have determined on the diabolical plan of seizing the first slight pretext to turn in the military, to butcher the prisoners for the gratification of his malice and revenge. It unfortunately happened, that in the afternoon of the 6th of April, some boys who were playing ball in No. 7 yard, knocked their ball over into the barrack-yard, and on the sentry in that yard refusing to throw it back to them, they picked a hole in the wall to get in after it.

This afforded Shortland his wished-for pretext, and he took his measures accordingly; he had all the garrison drawn up in the military walk, additional numbers posted on the walls, and every thing ready prepared before the alarm bell was rung; this, he naturally concluded, would draw the attention of a great number of prisoners towards the gates, to learn the cause of the alarm, while the turnkeys were despatched into the yards to lock all the doors but one of each prison, to prevent the prisoners retreating out of the way before he had sufficiently wreaked his vengeance.

What adds peculiar weight to the belief of its being a premeditated, determined massacre, are,

*First.*—The sanguinary disposition manifested on every occasion by Shortland, he having, prior to this time, ordered the soldiers to fire into the prisons, through the prison windows, upon unarmed prisoners asleep in their hammocks, on account of a light being seen in the prisons; which barbarous act was repeated several nights successively. That murder was not then committed, was owing to an over-ruling Providence alone; for the balls were picked up in the prison, where they passed through the hammocks of men then asleep in them. He having also ordered the soldiers to fire upon the prisoners in the yard of No. 7 prison, because they would not deliver up to him a man who had escaped from the *cachot*, which order the commanding officer of the soldiers refused to obey; and generally, he having seized on every slight pretext to injure the prisoners, by stopping their marketing for ten days repeatedly, and once a third part of their provisions for the same length of time.

*Secondly.*—He having been heard to say, when the boys had picked the hole in the wall, and some time before the alarm bell rung, while all the prisoners were quiet as usual in their respective yards, *"I'll fix the damn'd rascals directly."*

*Thirdly.*—His having all the soldiers on their posts, and the garrison fully prepared before the alarm bell rung. It could not then, of course, be rung to assemble the soldiers, but to alarm the prisoners, and create confusion among them.

*Fourthly.*—The soldiers upon the wall, previous to the alarm bell being rung, informing the prisoners that they would be charged upon directly.

*Fifthly.*—The turnkeys going into the yards and closing all the doors but one in each prison, while the attention of the prisoners was attracted by the alarm bell. This was done about fifteen minutes sooner than usual, and without informing the prisoners it was time to shut up. It was ever the invariable practice of the turnkeys, from which they never deviated before that night, when coming into the yard to shut up, to hollow to the prisoners so loud as to be heard throughout the yards, *"turn in, turn in!"* but, on that night, it was done so secretly, that not one man in a hundred knew they were shut; and in particular their shutting the door of No. 7 prison, which the prisoners usually went in and out at, [and which was formerly always closed last] and leaving one open in the other end of the prison, which was exposed to a cross-fire from the soldiers on the walls, and which the prisoners had to pass in gaining the prisons.

We here solemnly aver, that there was no preconcerted plan to attempt breaking out. There cannot be produced the least shadow of a reason or inducement for that intention, the prisoners daily expecting to be released, and to embark on board cartels for their native country. And we likewise solemnly assert, that there was no intention of resisting, in any manner, the authority of this depot.

N. B. Seven were killed, thirty dangerously wounded, and thirty slightly so. Total, sixty-seven killed and wounded.

(Signed)

WM. B. ORNE,        }

WM. HOBART,       }

JAMES BOGGS,           }

JAMES ADAMS,           }

FRANCIS JOSEPH,        }

JOHN F. TROBRIDGE, } *Committee.*

JOHN RUST,             }

HENRY ALLEN,           }

WALTER COLTON,         }

THOMAS B. MOTT.        }

DARTMOOR PRISON, April 7th, 1815.

The same day Mr. Ingraham come to the prison and informed the prisoners that he had come for the purpose of shipping a number of men, to man ships now lying in different ports in Europe; he also informed us that he had been appointed agent, under the consular agent of the United States: and that every preparation was making for the immediate release of every prisoner, and we might be assured of the immediate arrival of the ships from London to convey us to the United States.

On the tenth, a number were discharged to man different ships in Europe; this day arrangements were made by the prisoners, for the assistance and relief of our wounded countrymen in the Hospital, and also an arrangement for the prisoners to wear crape on their arm for thirty days after their arrival in America, as a tribute of respect due to their departed friends and fellow-prisoners. The wounded in the hospital were paid every attention, for their comfort and speedy recovery, by Doctor Magrath.

We received no letters from Mr. Beasley, although hundreds of letters had been sent to him since the melancholy event of the 6th. Reports were circulating that a new agent was to be appointed by the United States to supersede Mr. Beasley, which every man most anxiously wished might be true, but had not the satisfaction to learn it was the case; every day's delay made more confusion and anxiety among the prisoners. The weather during this month up to the present day, had been remarkably fine, pure and healthy, and more so than it had been at this place since our confinement; as if the All-Seeing Eye of Heaven looked down with pity and compassion upon our injured and wounded countrymen, and dispensed His blessings for their speedy recovery in the salubrity of His air. That passage in Holy Writ, in this instance, seemed to be remarkably verified: "that when the prisoner was sick in prison, He visited him."

Capt. Shortland, after being acquitted, resumed the command of the depot, but he was seldom seen by the prisoners, being very apprehensive that the prisoners would shoot him the first opportunity; therefore he kept a body guard around him, and this day a draft of thirty prisoners being discharged, and having to pass by his house, he had his guard stationed at his door.

On the morning of the twelfth, we were informed by Capt. Shortland that the drafts for the discharge of the prisoners were already made out, and that the draft for the first cartel would consist of 280, to be discharged as they entered this depot. I therefore obtained the exact number of prisoners then in each prison, which I shall give as follows:

| | |
|---|---|
| Prison No 1, contained, | 1290 |
| 3, | 952 |
| 4, | 978 |
| 5, | 938 |
| 7, | 1248 |
| In different employments about the stores and hospital, | 29 |
| Patients in the hospital, | 107 |
| | ———— |
| Total number of unparoled prisoners in England, | 5542 |

In visiting the hospitals, I found the wounded prisoners fast recovering, all in high spirits, the prison generally more healthy than it had been since our arrival in it. Capt. Shortland removed his family from this place, for his guilt had brought upon him the apprehension of the first draught's retaliating upon him by attacking his family; but no such idea had entered the imagination of any prisoner; it was the creature of his own guilt.

We were ordered at this time to be in readiness to deliver up every article which we had received from the British Government; such as beds, hammocks, blankets, &c., &c. These articles had been in our possession, and in constant use ever since the second of April, 1813, and had never been changed; we felt but little reluctance in delivering them up, when animated with the idea of once more visiting our native country, and leaving a dreary prison, which many of us had inhabited for upwards of two years.

On the following day we received a London paper which contained the following account of the late horid massacre at this depot; it read as follows:

An affair of a serious nature has recently taken place at Dartmoor prison: the prisoners attaching the greater part of the fault of their long detention since the peace, to Mr. Beasley their country's agent, resident at London, had, before the affray, burnt his person in effigy in the yard of their prison; on account of which, Captain Shortland, unarmed and unattended, entered the yard of their prison with a view to appease the anger of these unfortunate men; but his reception was attended with the prisoners discharging a pistol at him, the contents of which grazed his clerk; upon this the prisoners attempted to gain their liberty by rushing out of the gates, but were soon coiled by the guards firing upon them, and killing twelve, and wounding thirty.

The account was equally base and false, as the act was cruel and murderous; but the mention of twelve killed confirmed the prisoners in their belief that this number had been killed, and the five which were not to be found, were secretly buried by Captain Shortland that night, and that he, in the guilty and confused state of his mind, had given an account of twelve instead of seven, which were the only ones found of the killed. I leave it to the reader to judge whether nature or habit had done most towards hardening the feelings of this man. It is well known that men accustomed to the sufferings and misery of their fellow-beings, soon grow hardened and forget them. But could this man from the short time here, have grown so callous in his feelings as to commit such acts from habit, or must cruelty and malice have been woven in his constitution?

On this day, the prisoners in making preparation for their departure, prepared a large white flag, and as a memento had in the middle of it, the representation of a tomb, with the Goddess of Liberty leaning on it, and a murdered sailor lying by its side, and an inscription over it in large capital letters, "*Columbia weeps, and we remember.*" This flag was intended to be carried home to the United States, as it showed a just resentment for the execrable deeds which it recorded, and a just respect for the sufferers. This same day, numbers of prisoners were released by application of their friends in England, for the purpose of manning ships in different ports. We had no news from Mr. Beasley, and most of the prisoners barefooted, the oldest in a state of nudity, not having received any jackets or trowsers for more than eleven months.

At length, when we were almost dead with impatience and delay, on the fourteenth we received a letter from Mr. Beasley to the following effect:

Fellow Citizens,

I have been informed that numbers of the prisoners have entertained an idea that they are to remain in prison, until the arrival of some United States' ships in this country; but I can assure them that there is no foundation for the belief; and I can assure them of eight cartels being already taken up for their conveyance to the United States. And with regret I hear from officers who were sent to inquire into the shameful conduct of the sixth of April, that the extravagant excess of the prisoners was partly occasioned by their censuring the United States and myself.

Mr. Beasley had, no doubt, been informed of what he wrote, but it was not the fact, for his information, no doubt, came from the two officers who were here, the Admiral and his associate; but no such conversation took place in their hearing, which numbers of the most respectable prisoners can testify, and no such idea had been entertained by any prisoner in the prison. These officers intended that Mr. Beasley should bear all the blame. God knows his conduct was blameable enough throughout; but to do him justice he had no blame in the murderous act of the fatal sixth of April. His effigy had been burnt on the 24th of March, and all animosity had been dissipated with the ashes of his effigy, and his name seemed to be forgotten, for it was scarcely ever mentioned. Mr. Beasley had had every particular of the event before his interview with the officers, but made no exertions as yet to inquire into the affray.

The weather up to this day since the month began, had been remarkably fine for this place, but this morning the moor, as far as the eye could reach, was covered with snow, and continued to snow all day, and the weather very cold.

On the sixteenth we received letters from London, from many of our fellow-citizens, who had received passports and left the prison since the fatal sixth of April; on their arrival in London, they were taken before the lord mayor of that city, and their depositions taken relative to the massacre of the sixth, which was to the same purport as before the committee. On the same day, Col. Hawker, formerly consular agent, under the American consul at London, visited the prison for the purpose of shipping seamen to man ships at Plymouth, bound to New-Orleans. In this way the prisoners were daily diminishing in number, as any one might obtain a passport who could procure a friend to make application for their release, and informing Mr. Beasley that they required no assistance from him to convey them to the United States. In obtaining a passport in this way from Capt. Shortland, they needed no other protection in this country.

This day a man was committed to the cachot for drawing money from Col. Hawker in an assumed name. The colonel was determined to have him brought to condign punishment: this man the next day was taken out of the cachot and conveyed to Exeter, to be tried at the next August assizes.

On visiting the hospital, I found the wounded and the sick fast recovering, and had every attention paid them by Dr. Magrath, for their health and comfort, that his resources would allow.

On the seventeenth, a black man belonging to No. 4 was found dead in his hammock. On this day we received another letter from Mr. Beasley, which informed us that those officers who had visited the prison by order of the British government, had represented the conduct of the prisoners on the sixth of April, in a very unfavorable light, but having received a correct statement from the prison, and a general summary of the evidence on both sides as delivered in to the jury of inquest; he now apologized for his last letter.

On the nineteenth, at four o'clock in the afternoon, an express arrived informing Capt. Shortland that one cartel had arrived at Plymouth, and ordered him immediately to remove two hundred and forty-nine prisoners from this depot to that place, for embarking on board the ship. At five in the afternoon, the whole draft was collected in the square, with all their baggage. This was the first draft of prisoners that had entered the prison after the declaration of war, and had been immured within these gloomy walls more than two long and tedious years. They were then informed that one baggage wagon would be allowed to every hundred men, for the convenience of their baggage to Plymouth.

The prisoners being the greater part barefooted, made inquiry whether any arrangement had been made by Mr. Beasley for providing them with shoes and clothes, as they were much in want of them; but were much surprised and disappointed when they found no provision had been made. The money due from government had run over the usual time of payment, now twenty-five days, although application had previously been made for the payment of the daily allowance, and also, the other articles, both by the prisoners and Capt. Shortland himself; but Mr. Beasley still neglected to make any arrangement for either.

At six every prisoner's name was called, and they committed together with their baggage to a separate prison, ready for their departure the next morning. The joy they felt on this occasion is better imagined than described; I therefore leave to the imagination of the reader, what emotions the heart must feel, when a change which promised every endearment of life to them, and freed them from every evil of it, was about to take place.

I visited the hospital this evening for the last time, and had the pleasing satisfaction of finding the sick and wounded in a state of fast recovery, except a few who were dangerous.

The next morning we took our departure for Plymouth, and with joy in our hearts bid farewell to that pale of misery, and at four in the afternoon arrived at Plymouth, having travelled all the way under the direction of a strong guard.

We were immediately embarked on board the cartel Maria Christiana, a Swedish ship, commanded by Capt. Dirkes; we found some few of our countrymen who had been on parole, on board the ship.

It was now just forty days since the arrival of the ratified treaty in England.

The next day eight of the prisoners left the cartel to join a brig under French colors bound for France.

On the twenty-second the wind being contrary, the prisoners were permitted to go on shore and spend the day. A court of inquiry had been instituted by commissioners appointed by both governments, for the investigation of the unfortunate occurrences of the sixth of April, and was then sitting for that purpose. Several of the prisoners were called upon to give evidence in the cause, and their depositions taken by the court that day.

The court was attended by Mr. Williams, deputy consular agent to Mr. Beasley.

Before we set sail Mr. Williams informed us that he was instructed by Mr. Beasley to take down all the particulars of the investigation, for the purpose of laying them before the American government; but the commissioners had not reported when we left Plymouth, but it was expected they would in a few days, which shall constitute a part of this work as soon as it is received.

Mr. Williams informed us that the money allowed by government, which had been due thirty days, would not be paid by Mr. Beasley, nor would any provision be made by him for shoes or clothing, but that the prisoners must go home as they were.

On the twenty-third, the wind being favorable, we hove short, and made preparations for sailing.

On mustering the prisoners, we found their number amounted to two hundred and sixty-three; this increase of number was by officers paroled at Ashburton.

At three in the afternoon we left the port of Plymouth, with a fresh and favorable wind.

We had left behind at Dartmoor five thousand one hundred and ninety-three of our fellow prisoners, whom the agent informed us would be conveyed to this place in the same manner as ourselves in a few days, as the other cartels were on their way round to Plymouth, and thence to embark immediately for the United States. After leaving Plymouth we found the provisions under the direction of Capt. Turner, appointed by the agents to deal out the rations to the prisoners.

We were allowed, five days in the week, one pound of salt beef, one pound of bread, half a pound of potatoes a day; the other two days one pound of pork, the same quantity of bread, and half a pint of peas per man, and half a pint of vinegar a week.

Mr. Beasley had made arrangements for each prisoner to have a small bed and blanket; the cartel was equipped according to custom, with great guns and small arms.

A Physician had been appointed with a sufficient quantity of medicine to serve during the passage.

One part of the ship was allotted to the sick, where every attention was paid them by their countrymen for their comfort and convenience.

During the residue of the month nothing material occurred; cartel quite healthy, only five cases of sick, and them not very dangerous; the month ended with winds, light and unfavorable.

On the first of May we were in lat. 45° North, and longitude 23° 41' West. On the second, being in long. 24°, we spoke a brig from London bound to Quebec.

From the first to the fourteenth the winds were from N. W. to S. W., and the cartel kept between the latitudes of 42° and 44° North.

Some few sick but not dangerously. On this day we discovered a sail on our weather beam, standing to the eastward; at 2 P. M. she bore up and stood for the cartel, with a British flag flying; at four we spoke her in lat. 42, and long. 38. She proved to be a British transport with a number of troops from Mobile, bound to England, and fourteen days from Bermuda. She sent her boat alongside of the cartel with a naval and military officer, and the captain of the transport; they came on board the cartel and remained for an hour, and then returned to the transport, and each ship made sail for their destined places.

The winds still continued the same way the twenty-eighth. This day, Sunday, we fell in with several large islands of Ice, lat. 43°; on the same day, lat. 42° long. 60°, we spoke the brig Sally Barker, six days from Boston, bound for Portugal; the three days following the winds continuing light, from the South and West, we spoke a brig from Portland four days out, bound to Surinam.

Cartel perfectly healthy, with the exception of one man very low in a consumption.

On the first of June, lat. 40, 50, long. 64, spoke the ship Helvitius, of Philadelphia, bound home, after remaining during the whole war up the east country. On the 2nd of June, lat. 40, 35, long. 69, the majority of the prisoners agreed to take possession of the cartel, and run her into New-York, for the following reasons: the ship being disabled by the loss of her main trussel-trees, which endangered the top-mast, and rendered her unfit for sea; secondly, there being every appearance of a gale from the S. W. and the weather thick and hazy; thirdly, the port of New-York being the most convenient for the greater part of the prisoners; for which reasons, at twelve meridian, by the general voice of all on board, the command was taken from her former captain, and she directed for the port of New-York. At 4 P. M. the man in a consumption "put off this mortal coil," and took his quietus in thirty-five fathoms of water, in the usual form at sea.

The captain of the ship required some document, that he might show for his indemnification for resigning the command of the ship, and deviating from his destined port, which was Norfolk, Vir.; the following certificate, signed by a great number of the prisoners, was delivered him.

### CERTIFICATE.

We, the undersigned, citizens of the United States of America, do hereby certify, that on the second day of June, 1815, at twelve meridian, being in lat. 40, 30, long. 69, 30, by mutual agreement of a majority of prisoners now on board the cartel Maria Christiana, bound for Norfolk, did take possession of her, and directed her for the port of New-York.

At four o'clock on the third, we discovered the highland of New-Jersey bearing W. by S.; at eight made the light house, distance three or four leagues; at two P. M. obtained a pilot and stood within the Hook; at seven came to an anchor; the next morning arrived at New-York.

Having received the report of the commissioners since our arrival in the United States, we shall give it to the reader verbatim. The reader will perceive that it differs somewhat from the account of the massacre which I have given before, and that of the committee of prisoners. The public are to judge of the report; the facts seemed not to warrant just such an one; but to give my simple opinion as an individual, I believe that the commissioners, through a sort of *pia fraus* for the love of peace and harmony between the two governments, have made it a vail of amnesty, and a preventative of new troubles.

## THE REPORT OF THE COMMISSIONERS.

PLYMOUTH, 26th April, 1815.

We, the undersigned commissioners, appointed on behalf of our respective governments, to inquire into, and report upon, the unfortunate occurrence of the 6th of April instant, at Dartmoor prison, having carefully perused the proceedings of the several courts of inquiry instituted immediately after that event, by the orders of Admiral Sir John T. Duckworth and Major General Brown respectively, as well as the depositions taken at the coroner's inquest upon the bodies of the prisoners who lost their lives upon that melancholy occasion; upon which inquest the jury found a verdict of justifiable homicide; proceed immediately to the examination upon oath, in the presence of one or more of the magistrates of the vicinity, of all the witnesses, both American and English, who offered themselves for that purpose, or who could be discovered as likely to afford any material information upon the subject, as well as those who had been previously examined before the coroner, or otherwise, to the number in the whole of about eighty. We further proceed to a minute examination of the prisons, for the purpose of clearing up some points, which upon the evidence alone, were scarcely intelligible; obtaining from the prisoners, and from the officers of the depot, all the necessary assistance and explanation; and premising, that we have been from necessity compelled to draw many of our conclusions from statements and evidence highly contradictory, we do now make upon the whole proceedings the following report:

During the period which has elapsed since the arrival in this country of the account of the ratification of the treaty of Ghent, an increased degree of restlessness and impatience of confinement appears to have prevailed amongst the American prisoners at Dartmoor, which, though not exhibited in the shape of any violent excess, has been principally indicated by threats of breaking out if not soon released.

On the fourth of this month in particular, only two days previous to the events, the subject of this inquiry, a large body of the prisoners rushed into the market-square, from whence, by the regulations of the prison, they are excluded, demanding bread, instead of bircuit, which had on that day been issued by the officers of the depot; their demands, however, having been then almost immediately complied with, they returned to their own yards, and the employment of force on that occasion became unnecessary.

On the evening of the sixth, about six o'clock, it was clearly proved to us, that a breach had been made in one of the prison walls, sufficient for a full-sized man to pass, and that others had been commenced in the course of the day near the same spot, though never completed.

That a number of the prisoners were over the railing erected to prevent them from communicating with the sentinels on the walls, which was of course forbidden by the regulations of the prison, and that in the space between the railing and those walls, they were tearing up pieces of turf, and wantonly pelting each other in a noisy and disorderly manner.

That a much more considerable number of the prisoners was collected together at that time in one of their yards near the place where the breach was effected, and that although such collection of prisoners was not unusual at other times (the gambling tables being commonly kept in that part of the yard) yet, when connected with the circumstances of the breach, and the time of the day, which was after the hour the signal for the prisoners to their respective prisons had ceased to sound, it became a natural and just ground of alarm to those who had charge of the depot.

It was also in evidence that in the building formerly the petty officers' prison, but now the guard barrack, which stands in the yard to which the hole in the wall would serve as a communication, a part of the arms of the guard who were off duty, were usually kept in the racks, and though there was no evidence that this was in any respect the motive which induced the prisoners to make the opening in the wall, or even that they were ever acquainted with the fact, it naturally became at least a further cause of suspicion and alarm, and an additional reason for precaution.

Upon these grounds, Captain Shortland appears to us to have been justified in giving the order, which about this time he seems to have given, to sound the alarm-bell, the usual signal for collecting the officers of the depot, and putting the military on the alert.

However reasonable and justifiable this was as a measure of precaution, the effects produced thereby in the prisons, but which could not have been intended, were most unfortunate, and deeply to be regretted. A considerable number of the prisoners in the yards, where no disturbances existed before, and who were either already within their respective prisons, or quietly retiring as usual towards them, immediately upon the sound of the bell rushed back from curiosity (as it appears) towards the gates, where, by that time, the crowd had assembled, and many who were at the time absent from their yards, were also, from the plan of the prison, compelled, in order to reach their own homes, to pass by the same spot, and thus, that which was merely a measure of precaution, in its operation increased the evil it was intended to prevent.

Almost at the same instant that the alarm-bell rang, (but whether before or subsequent, is, upon the evidence, doubtful, though Captain Shortland states it positively, as one of his further reasons for causing it to ring) some one or more of the prisoners broke the iron chain, which was the only fastening of No. 1 gate, leading into the market-square, by means of an iron bar; and a very considerable number of the prisoners immediately rushed towards that gate; and many of them began to press forwards as fast as the opening would permit, into the square.

There was no direct proof before us of previous concert or preparation on the part of the prisoners; and no evidence of their intention or disposition to effect their escape on this occasion, excepting that which arose by inference from the whole of the above detailed circumstances connected together.

The natural and almost irresistible inference to be drawn, however, from the conduct of the prisoners by Captain Shortland and the military, was, that an intention on the part of the prisoners to escape was on the point of being carried into execution, and it was at least certain that they were by force passing beyond the limits prescribed to them, at a time when they ought to have been quietly going in for the night. It was also in evidence that the outer gates of the market-square were usually opened about this time to let the bread-wagon pass and repass to the store, although at the period in question they were in fact closed.

Under these circumstances, and with these impressions necessarily operating upon his mind, and a knowledge that if the prisoners once penetrated through the square, the power of escape was almost to a certainty afforded to them, if they should be so disposed. Capt. Shortland, in the first instance, proceeded down the square towards the prisoners, having ordered a part of the different guards, to the number of about fifty only at first, (though they were increased afterwards,) to follow him. For some time both he and Dr. Magrath endeavored by quiet means and persuasion, to induce the prisoners to retire to their own yards, explaining to them the fatal consequences which must ensue if they refused, as the military would in that case be necessarily compelled to employ force. The guard was by this time formed in the rear of Capt. Shortland, about two thirds of the way down the square—the latter is about one hundred feet broad, and the guard extended nearly all across. Captain Shortland, finding that persuasion was all in vain, and that although some were induced by it to make an effort to retire, others pressed on in considerable numbers, at last ordered about 15 file of the guard, nearly in front of the gate which had been forced, to charge the prisoners back to their own yards. The prisoners were in some places so near the military, that one of the soldiers states he could not come fairly down to the charge; and the military were unwilling to act as against an enemy. Some of the prisoners also were unwilling and reluctant to retire, and some pushing and struggling ensued between the parties, arising partly from intention, but mainly from the pressure of those behind preventing those in front from getting back. After some little time, however, this charge appears to have been so far effective, and that with little or no injury to the prisoners, as to have driven them for the most part quite down out of the square, with the exception of a small number who continued their resistance about No. 1 gate. A great crowd still remained collected after this in the passage between the square and the prisoners' yards, and in the part of these yards in the vicinity of the gates. This assemblage still refused to withdraw, and according to most of the English witnesses, and some of the American, was making a noise, hallooing, insulting and provoking, and daring the military to fire, and, according to the evidence of some of the soldiers, and some others, was pelting the military with large stones, by which some of them were actually struck. This circumstance is, however, denied by many of the American witnesses; and some of the English, upon having the question put to them, stated they saw no stones thrown previously to the firing, although their situation at the time was such as to enable them to see most of the other proceedings in the square. Under these circumstances the firing commenced. With regard to any order having been given to fire, the evidence is very contradictory. Several of the Americans swear positively that Capt. Shortland gave that order; but the manner in which, from the confusion of the moment, they describe this part of the transaction, is so different in its details, that it is very difficult to reconcile their testimony. Many of the soldiers and other English witnesses heard the word given by some one, but no one of them can swear it was by Capt. Shortland, or by any one in particular, and some, amongst whom is the officer commanding the guard, think, if Capt. Shortland had given such an order, that they must have heard it, which they did not. In addition to this, Capt. Shortland denies the fact; and from the situation in which he appears to have been placed at the time, even according to the American witnesses, in front of the soldiers, it may appear somewhat improbable that he should then have given such an order. But, however, it may remain a matter of doubt whether the firing first began in the square by order, or was a spontaneous act of the soldiers themselves, it seemed clear that it was continued and renewed both there and elsewhere, without orders; and that on the platforms, and in several places about the prison, it was certainly commenced without any authority. The fact of an order having been given at first, provided the firing was, under the existing circumstances, justifiable, does not appear very material in any other point of view than as showing a want of self-possession and discipline in the troops, if they should have fired without order. With regard to the above most important consideration, of whether the firing was justifiable or not, we are of opinion, under all the circumstances of the case, from the apprehension which the soldiers might fairly entertain, owing to the numbers and conduct of the prisoners, that this firing to a certain extent, was justifiable in a military point of view, in order to intimidate the prisoners, and compel them thereby to desist from all acts of violence, and to retire as they were ordered, from a situation in which the responsibility of the agents, and the military, could not permit them with safety to remain.—From the fact of the crowd being so close, and the firing at first being attended with very little injury, it appears probable that a large proportion of the muskets were, as stated by one or two of the witnesses, levelled over the heads of the prisoners; a circumstance in some respects to be lamented, as it induced them to cry out "blank cartridges," and merely irritated and encouraged them to renew their insults to the soldiery, which produced a repetition of the firing in a manner much more destructive. The firing in the square having continued for some time, by which several of the prisoners sustained injuries, the greater part of them appear to have been running back with the utmost precipitation and confusion to their respective prisons, and the cause for further firing seems at this period to have ceased. It appears accordingly that Capt. Shortland was in the market-square, exerting himself and giving orders to that effect, and that Lieut. Fortye had succeeded in stopping the fire of his part of the guard. Under these circumstances, it is very difficult to find any justification for the further continuance and renewal of the firing, which certainly took place both in the prison yards and elsewhere; though we have some evidence of subsequent provocation given to the military, and resistance to the turnkeys in shutting the prisons, and of stones being thrown out from within the prison doors. The subsequent firing rather appears to have arisen from the state of individual irritation and exasperation on the part of the soldiers who followed the prisoners into their yards, and from the absence of nearly all the officers, who might have restrained it; as well as from the great difficulty of putting an end to a firing when once commenced under such circumstances. Capt. Shortland was from this time busily occupied with the turnkeys in the square, receiving and taking care of the wounded. Ensign White remained with his guard at the breach, and Lieuts. Avelyne and Fortye, the only other subalterns known to have been present, continued in the square with the main bodies of their respective guards.

The time of the day, which was the officers' dinner hour, will, in some measure, explain this, as it caused the absence of every officer from the prison whose presence was not indispensable there. And this circumstance, which has been urged as an argument to prove the intention of the prisoners to take this opportunity to escape, tended to increase the confusion, and to prevent those great exertions being made, which might perhaps have obviated a portion, at least, of the mischief which ensued.

At the same time that the firing was going on in the square, a cross fire was also kept up from several of the platforms on the walls round the prison where the sentries stand, by straggling parties of soldiers who ran up there for that purpose. As far as this fire was directed to disperse the men assembled round the breach, for which purpose it was most effectual, it seems to stand upon the same ground as that in the first instance in the square. But that part, which it is positively sworn was directed against struggling parties of prisoners running about the yards and endeavoring to enter in the few doors which the turnkeys, according to their usual practice, had left open, does seem, as stated, to have been wholly without object or excuse, and to have been a wanton attack upon the lives of defenceless, and at that time unoffending individuals. In the same, or even more severe terms, we must remark upon what was proved as to the firing into the door-ways of the prisons, more particularly into that of No. 3 prison, at a time when the men were in crowds at the entrance. From the position of the prison and of the door, and from the marks of the balls which were pointed out to us, as well as from the evidence, it was clear this firing must have proceeded from soldiers a very few feet from the door-way; and although it was certainly sworn that the prisoners were at the time of part of the firing at least, continuing to insult and occasionally to throw stones at the soldiers, and that they were standing in the way of, and impeding the turnkey, who was there for the purpose of closing the door, yet still there was nothing stated which could in our view at all justify such excessively harsh and severe treatment of helpless and unarmed prisoners, when all idea of escape was at an end. Under these impressions we used every endeavor to ascertain if there was the least prospect of identifying any of the soldiers who had been guilty of the particular outrages here alluded to, or of tracing any particular death at that time to the firing of any particular individual, but without success; and all hopes of bringing the offenders to punishment should seem to be at an end. In conclusion, we, the undersigned, have only to add, that whilst we lament, as we do most deeply, the unfortunate transaction which has been the subject of this inquiry, we find ourselves totally unable to suggest any steps to be taken as to those parts of it which seem to call for redress and punishment.

(Signed)

CHARLES KING,
FRAS. SEYMOUR LARPENT.

—

LONDON, 18th April, 1815.

SIR,

At the request of Lord Castlereagh, we have had interviews with him and Mr. Goulburn on the subject of the transportation of the American prisoners now in this country, to the United States, and of the late unfortunate event at the depot at Dartmoor.

On the first subject we agreed to advise your acceptance of the proposition of Lord Castlereagh to transport the prisoners at the joint expense of the two countries, reserving the construction of the articles of the treaty, which provides for the mutual restoration of prisoners, for future adjustment. It was stated by us, and was so understood, that the joint expense, thus to be incurred, is to comprehend as well the requisite tonnage as the subsistence of the prisoners; and moreover that measures of precaution should be adopted relative to the health and comfort of the prisoners similar to those which had taken place in America.

The details of this arrangement, if you concur with us as to the expediency of making it, are left with you to settle with the proper British authority.

On the other subject, as a statement of the transaction has been received from the American prisoners, differing very materially in fact from that which had resulted from an inquiry instituted by the port admiral, it has been thought advisable that some means should be devised of procuring information as to the real state of the case, in order, on the one hand, to show that there had not been any wanton or improper sacrifice of the lives of American citizens, or, on the other, to enable the British government to punish their civil and military officers, if it should appear that they have resorted to measures of extreme severity without necessity, or with too much precipitation.

Lord Castlereagh proposed that the inquiry should be a joint one, conducted by a commissioner selected by each government. And we have thought such an inquiry most likely to produce an impartial and satisfactory result.

We presume that you will have too much occupation on the first subject and the other incidental duties of your office, to attend to this inquiry in person. On that supposition, we have stated to the British government that we should recommend to you the selection of Charles King, Esq. as a fit person to conduct it on behalf of the American government. If Mr. King will undertake the business, he will forthwith proceed to Dartmoor, and in conjunction with the British commissioner, who may be appointed on the occasion, will examine the persons concerned, and such other evidence as may be thought necessary, and make a joint report upon the facts of the case to John Q. Adams, Esq. Minister Plenipotentiary of the United States at this court, and to the British government.

The mode of executing this service must be left to the discretion of Mr. King and his colleague. If they can agree upon a narrative of the facts after having heard the evidence, it will be better than reporting the whole mass of testimony in detail, which they may perhaps find it necessary to do, if they cannot come to such an agreement.

We are, sir, your obedient humble servants,

(Signed)

H. CLAY,

ALBERT GALLATIN.

R. G. Beasley, Esq. &c., &c.

---

PLYMOUTH, 26th April, 1815.

SIR,

In pursuance of instructions received from Messrs. Clay and Gallatin, I have now the honor to transmit to you the report prepared by Mr. Larpent and myself on behalf of our respective governments, in relation to the unfortunate transactions at Dartmoor Prison of War, on the 6th of the present month. Considering it of much importance that the report, whatever it might be, should go forth under our joint signatures, I have forborne to press some of the points which it involves, as far as otherwise I might have done, and it therefore may not be improper in this letter to enter into some little explanation of such parts of the report. Although it does appear that a part of the prisoners were on that evening in such a state, and under such circumstances, as to have justified, in the view which the commander of the depot could not but take of it, the intervention of the military force, and even in a strict sense, the first use of fire-arms, yet I cannot but express it as my settled opinion, that by conduct a little more temporizing, this dreadful alternative of firing upon unarmed prisoners might have been avoided. Yet as this opinion has been the result of subsequent examination, and after having acquired a knowledge of the comparatively harmless state of the prisoners, it may be but fair to consider, whether in such a moment of confusion and alarm, as that appears to have been, the officer commanding could have fairly estimated his danger, or have measured out with precision the extent and nature of the force necessary to guard against it.

But when the firing became general, as it afterwards appears to have done, and caught with electric rapidity from the square to the platforms, there is no plea or shadow of excuse for it, except in the personal exasperation of the soldiery, nor for the more deliberate, and therefore more unjustifiable, firing which took place into three of the prisons, No. 1, 3 and 4, but more particularly into No. 3, after the prisoners had retired into them, and there was no longer any pretence of apprehensions as to their escape. Upon this ground, as you, sir, will perceive by the report, Mr. Larpent and myself had no difference of opinion, and I am fully persuaded that my own regret was not greater than his, at perceiving how hopeless would be the attempt to trace to any individuals of the military these outrageous proceedings.

As to whether the order to fire came from Captain Shortland, I yet confess myself unable to form any satisfactory opinion, though perhaps the bias of my mind is, that he did give such an order. But his anxiety and exertions to stop it after it had continued for some little time, are fully proved, and his general conduct, previous to this occurrence, as far as we could with propriety enter into such details, appears to have been characterized with great fairness, and even kindness, in the light in which he stood towards the prisoners.

On the subject of any complaints against their own government existing among the prisoners, it was invariably answered to several distinct questions put by me on that head, that none whatsoever existed or had been expressed by them, although they confessed themselves to entertain some animosity against Mr. Beasley, to whom they attributed their detention in this country; with what justice you, sir, will be better able to judge. They made no complaint whatsoever, as to their provisions and general mode of living and treatment in the prison.

I have transmitted to Mr. Beasley a list of the killed and wounded on this melancholy occasion, with a request that he would forward it to the United States for the information of their friends at home, and I am pleased to have it in my power to say, that the wounded are for the most part doing well.

I have also enclosed to Mr. Beasley the notes taken by me of the evidence adduced before us, with a request that he would have them fairly copied, as also a copy of the depositions taken before the coroner, and desired him to submit them to you when in order.

I cannot conclude, sir, without expressing my high sense of the impartiality and manly firmness with which this inquiry has been conducted on the part of Mr. Larpent, nor without mentioning that every facility was afforded to us in its prosecution, as well by the military officers commanding here and at the prison, as by the magistrates in the vicinity.

I have the honor to be, with much respect, your most obedient humble servant,

(Signed)

## CHARLES KING.

His Excellency, J. Q. ADAMS, &c., &c.

––––––––––––––

LONDON, 30th April, 1815.

SIR:

In my letter of the 19th instant, I informed you of the measures which had been adopted here in consequence of the late unfortunate event at Dartmoor prison.


I have now the honor to transmit the copy of a letter addressed to me by Mr. Clay and Mr. Gallatin, relative to that occurrence, and to the transportation of the American prisoners in this country to the United States.

In the absence of Mr. Adams, it becomes my duty to communicate, for the information of our government, the result of the investigation at Dartmoor. I enclose a copy of the joint report of the commissioners appointed for that purpose, also of a letter from Mr. King to Mr. Adams, and of a list of the killed and wounded on that melancholy occasion.

I shall leave to Mr. Adams any further steps which he may deem it proper to take in this business. I cannot, however, forbear to notice the erroneous impression of the prisoners, that their detention so long has been owing to me. You are aware, sir, of my constant exertions during the war to effect their liberation. I immediately, on the signing of the treaty of peace at Ghent, renewed my instances on that subject; proposing, as a condition, that all prisoners who might be delivered over to me by the British government, should be considered as prisoners of war, and not at liberty to serve until regularly exchanged, in the event of the treaty not being ratified by the President. This proposition was declined, and in a peremptory manner.

On the receipt of the intelligence of the ratification from America, I lost not a moment in requesting the release of the prisoners, according to the terms of the treaty; and the number of vessels which I had hired, as mentioned in my letter of the 13th, and which are now on their voyage to the United States, will show that the necessary steps were taken to provide for their immediate transportation to their country. The prisoners also were informed of these measures, and of the exertions which had been made from the commencement, to return them to their homes with the least possible delay. Therefore, whatever may have been their uneasiness, under confinement, and whatever hostile feelings they may have had towards me, as noticed in the report, and in Mr. King's letter, I must say, with confidence, that I could not prevent the one, nor have I deserved the other.

I have the honor to be, sir, your most obedient humble servant,

R. G. BEASLEY.

The Hon. JOHN MASON, &c. &c.

---

[From the Plymouth (Eng.) Telegraph, April 22, 1815.]

To                                    the                                    Editor.

SIR,

The officers and prisoners of this depot, feeling an ardent desire that the citizens of the United States may be informed of the many and great services rendered them by Dr. Magrath, and likewise that the subjects of Great Britain may learn with what sentiments of gratitude and respect his unparalleled efforts in the cause of humanity, and the discharge of his duty, have, at this depot, filled us; we have to request that you will cause to be inserted in your paper, as early as possible, copies of the enclosed testimonials, addressed to that gentleman.

I am, &c.,

BENJAMIN MERCER.

HOSPITAL, April 13, 1815.

---

DARTMOOR PRISON, March 28, 1815.

To His Excellency JAMES MADISON.

*Honored and respected Sir:*

From the general philanthrophy of your character, and liberality of sentiment, no apology is deemed requisite for introducing to your particular notice, and that of the nation at large, Dr. George Magrath, principal of the medical department for the American prisoners of war in England. It is impossible for us to speak of this gentleman in terms that will do justice to his superior professional science, brilliant talents, the exemplary virtues of his heart, the urbanity and easy accessibility of his manners, his unremitting assiduities and unwearied exertions, in combatting a succession of diseases of the most exasperated and malignant character, which prevailed among the prisoners. At the first forming of the depot, *pneumonia*, in its worst form, generally prevailed, which degenerated into a still more dangerous species of pulmonic complaint, nearly *peripneumonia notha*, which was rapidly succeeded by a putrid kind of measles, and that destructive malady followed by a malignant small-pox, which spread rapidly; dismay and apprehension were painted on every countenance.

Dr. Magrath's time and attention were fully occupied in the hospital, and in vaccinating the prisoners. From his unprecedented exertions in an inclement season of the year, in a most inhospitable clime, his health became seriously impaired; but totally regardless of himself, he persevered in his unparalleled exertions, and from his superior knowledge in the healing art, was the means, under divine Providence, of rescuing many citizens of the United States from the fast approximating embraces of death. This malignant species of small-pox, unknown to the generality of professional gentlemen, appeared in other places, and a far greater number fell victims, in proportion to the cases at the place. We therefore trust, that some distinguished mark of the nation's gratitude will be conferred on Dr. Magrath; for this truly great man's exertions in the cause of suffering humanity, have been rarely equalled, but never excelled.

We have the honor to remain, with sentiments of respect and attachment, your excellency's obedient humble servants,

| | |
|---|---|
| BENJ. MERCER, | } |
| PIERRE G. DE PEYSTER, | } |
| HENRY PROCTOR, | } |
| JOHN COTTLE, | } |
| THOS. CARBERRY, | } Hospital |
| JAMES LESTER, | } Committee. |
| HENRY BULL, | } |
| THOS. B. MOTT, | } |
| SETH WALKER, | } |
| WILLIAM WEST, | } For and in behalf of |
| CHARLES DEXTER, | } the Amer. prisoners |

WILLIAM MOLLEY,      } at this depot.

JOHN S. TROUBRIDGE,  }

HENRY SHERBURNE,     }

THOS. B. FROST.          }

---

## ANSWER.

*Officers and brave Americans collectively:*

Permit me to request you will accept the warmest and most sincere thanks of my heart, for the flattering testimonials of your approbation of my conduct, with which you have honored me, and allow me to assure you, that nothing can be more exquisitely gratifying to my very best feeling, than the language in which you have been pleased to convey this mark of your esteem. I feel convinced that you will indulgently excuse me, if I find it impossible to command words sufficiently emphatic, adequately to express the sentiments of gratitude, with which I am penetrated, for this unexpected proof of your regard; I must therefore allow my heart, rather than my pen, to thank you. But it would not be doing justice to my feelings were I to abstain from assuring you, that I have endeavored to perform my duty towards you, with that self-devotedness which looks only for its reward in its own consciousness of right, and its own secret sense of virtue; and whatever difficulties I have had to encounter in the discharge of my important trust, by struggling with a succession of the most violent and exasperated epidemic diseases, perhaps ever recorded in medical history, during the whole of my service among you, the distinguished proof of your confidence, and approbation of my professional labors, with which you this day have been pleased to honor me, amply compensates me, and must rank amongst the proudest and happiest events of my life. It now only remains for me, in this plain, but unfeigned language, again to beg you will receive my most sincere thanks; and to assure you, collectively, that a due and lively sense of the high honor which you have conferred upon me, shall, to the last moments of my existence, remain ingrafted in my breast. And here allow me most sincerely to congratulate you on the happy event which terminates your captivity, and which is soon to restore you to the bosoms of your families and friends; and that you may all enjoy peace and happiness, is the sincere wish of your most grateful and much obliged humble servant,

GEO. MAGRATH.

DARTMOOR, March 30, 1815.

DARTMOOR PRISON, April 9th, 1815.

To His Excellency JOHN Q. ADAMS.

SIR:

Impressed with the sense of duty which we owe to our country and to ourselves, we respectively solicit permission to introduce to your Excellency George Magrath, Esq., M.D., principal of the medical department at this depot. Language is incompetent to delineate the worth and character of this gentleman, pre-eminent in medical science, enriched by every virtue and accomplishment that can dignify and adorn human nature, and form the gentleman and philanthrophist.

His professional skill has been peculiarly conspicuous in his successfully combatting a succession of diseases, of the most exasperated and malignant character, which prevailed among the prisoners.

Dr. Magrath's health, from his indefatigable exertions, became seriously impaired, but he persevered in the performance of his arduous duties and unremitting efforts to arrest the alarming and rapid advances of the prevailing diseases; and he was the agent under divine Providence of rescuing many citizens of the United States from a premature grave, and as it were, renewing their existence, but more particularly on the late unhappy occurrence.

Language is too impotent to describe Dr. Magrath's unexampled endeavors to prevent the effusion of blood; regardless of the many dangers by which he was environed, he persevered, amidst the heavy and incessant fire of musketry, in his humane endeavors to prevent the fatal catastrophe.

His treatment of the unfortunate wounded Americans is superior to all praise, and was such as to entitle Dr. Magrath to the esteem and gratitude of the citizens of the United States.

We therefore respectfully and ardently solicit that your Excellency would be pleased to honor Dr. Magrath with your particular notice and esteem, and to convey these our sentiments to the government of the United States; for we would wish to give all possible publicity to our high sense of Dr. Magrath, and to evince to our country and the world how gratefully we appreciate the essential services we have received from that gentleman.

We avail ourselves of this opportunity to offer to your Excellency our congratulations on the happy termination of your important duties at Ghent, by the conclusion of a peace so highly honorable to our beloved country, and to yourself, and to assure your Excellency of our high respect and attachment to your character and person.

We have the honor to be, Sir,

Your obedient humble servants,

For and in behalf of the American prisoners of war at this depot,

PIERRE G. DEPEYSTER,
HENRY PROCTOR,
HENRY BULL,
JOHN COTTLE,
THOS. GAIR,
THOS. CARBERRY,
JAMES LESTER,
BENJ. MERCER,
ISAAC DOWELL.

---

DARTMOOR, April 10, 1815.

GENTLEMEN,

Honored as I am with the approbation of those whose good opinion I so highly estimate, I cannot permit myself to receive this additional mark of your friendship and regard (in which you much overrate my humble exertions, in the discharge of my duty and the cause of humanity,) without begging leave to assure you, that whilst it reflects upon me the highest honor that could be conferred, it lays claim to my heartfelt acknowledgments and everlasting gratitude.

With the most sincere and cordial good wishes for your health and happiness,

I remain, gentlemen,

Your much obliged and most grateful servant,

GEO. MAGRATH.

To the gentlemen forming the Hospital Committee.

---

FEBRUARY, 1815.

*The following is a correct list of all who entered his Majesty's service out of Dartmoor prison from April 1813 until 1814; to which is annexed their former residence, and the ships in which they were captured or impressed.*

| | | |
|---|---|---|
| James Akin, | Roxbury, Mass., | Wm. Bayard. |
| Abel Akins, | Penobscot, Maine, | Tygris, Baltimore. |
| Alford Arnold, | unknown, Penn., | Viper, do |
| Wm. Armstrong, | Salem, Mass., | Rolla, priv. |
| Anthony Agusta, | New Orleans, | dodo |
| Henry Allen, | Roxbury, Mass., | Wm. Bayard, N. Y. |
| George Blanchard, | Elizabeth, N. J., | do |
| Gabriel Bugoine, | —— Vir., | brig Star, N. Y. |
| Henry Brown, | New York, | Criterion, Baltimore. |
| Edward Blackstone, | Kennebunk, Maine, | do |
| Wm. Bishop, | Danverse, Mass., | Spitfire, Boston. |
| Wm. Brown, | New-Point-Comfort, Vir., | U. S. brig Argus. |
| Frederick Cransburgh, | Prussia, | brig Star. |
| John C. Cox, | b. New York, | do |
| Stephen Churchell, | Richmond, Vir., | Viper, Balt. |
| Samuel Cook, | Tiverton, R. I., | Price, do |
| Albert Cooper, | Newburyport, Mass., | man-of-war. |
| Jerodia Denison, | Middleton, Con., | brig Star. |
| John Duncan, | Boston, | Viper. |
| Wm. Ervine, | New York, | Virginia Planter. |
| Francis Foster, | New London, Con., | Meteor, N. Y. |
| Shubel Folger, | Nantucket, Mass., | Wm. Bayard. |
| William Fenton, | Wiscasset, Maine, | man-of-war. |
| Daniel Holt, | New London, Con., | brig Star, N. Y. |
| John Hughs, | New York, | dodo |

| | | |
|---|---|---|
| John Hubbard, | do | dodo |
| James Holms, | Portsmouth, N. H., | Magdalin, N. Y. |
| Thomas Howell, | Beverley, Mass., | Independence. |
| Anthony Hughieco, | New Orleans, | Rolla, privateer. |
| Aaron Hinkley, | Bath, Mass., | Viper, Balt. |
| Francis Joseph, | New Orleans, | brig Star, N. Y. |
| James Jackson, | Phil., Penn., | Paul Jones, N. Y. |
| John Little, | do | Unknown |
| Mathew Latimore, | N. Y., | Meteor, N. Y. |
| Robert Murray, | Newport, R. I., | Rolla, Phil. |
| Henry Neal, | N. Y., N. Y., | Ned, Balt. |
| Charles M'Nites, | Balt., Maryland, | Ned, Balt. |
| John Newgen, | N. Y., | True-blooded Yankee. |
| Francis Rice, | Boston, Mass., | Virginia Planter. |
| Ebenezer Rich, | Portland, Mass., | Flash, N. Y. |
| John Senate, | Philadelphia, | Wm. Bayard. |
| John Sheard, | Poughkeepsie, N. Y., | do |
| John Shultz, | Denmark, | Criterion, N. Y. |
| Wm. Smith, | New York, | Terrible. |
| John Thompson, | Denmark, | brig Star. |
| Wm. Thomas, | Germany, | Viper, Balt. |
| Zach. Tough, | New London, Con., | Terrible. |
| John Williams, | New York, N. Y., | Wm. Bayard. |
| Edward Washburn, | New York, N. Y., | brig Star. |
| George Williams, | Balt., Maryl., | Charlotte, Charls. |
| John Wilson, | Phil., Penn., | Governor Gerry, N. Y. |
| William Warner, | New York, N. Y., | Ajax. |

| | | |
|---|---|---|
| John West, | dodo | Dukanor. |
| Israel Wright, | Tinmouth, Ver., | brig Star, N. Y. |
| Wm. Wilson, | Long Island, N. Y., | Ned, Balt. |
| Robert Wesel, | New York, do | do |
| James Pickerton, | Hampton, Vir., | Lightning, Phil. |
| Francis Lisda, | New Orleans, Louisiana, | Unknown. |
| James Johnson, | New York, N. Y., | brig Mars. |

------

*The following is a correct List of all who entered his Majesty's service from the different prison ships at Chatham, from April 1813, until June 1814. Copied from the clerk's books.*

| | | |
|---|---|---|
| John Anderson, | b. Newcastle, Del., | man-of-war. |
| John Atkinson, | b. Baltimore, Maryland, | True Blood. |
| John Austin, | unknown, | unknown. |
| Josiah Abraham, | Phil., Penn., | man-of-war. |
| James Anderson, | Balt., Maryland, | unknown. |
| Peter Boyd, | New York, N. Y., | do |
| John Boyd, | Kennebunk, Mass., | do |
| John Brown, | New Bedford, | Impressed. |
| John Bauld, | Block Island, | man-of-war. |
| Isaac Baily, | Boston, Mass., | do |
| John Brown, | Salem, do | True Blood. |
| Peter Brown, | Phil., Penn., | unknown. |
| George Bing, | New York, N. Y., | man-of-war. |
| John Brown, | b. Salem, Mass., | do |
| Samuel Billham, | b. do do | do |
| John Barks, | New Bedford, | do |
| George Burns, | Phil., Penn., | do |

| | | |
|---|---|---|
| Asa Bumpus, | New Bedford, Mass., | unknown. |
| Rufus Brown, | Eastport, | do |
| John Burns, | North Carolina, | do |
| John Baily, | Hainsbury, Mass., | do |
| Ebenezer Carter, | Portsmouth, N. H., | man-of-war. |
| Isaac Crawford, | Boston, Mass., | do |
| Benjamin Cotton, | Norfolk, Vir., | man-of-war. |
| Thomas Charles, | b. New York, N. Y., | do |
| Charles Cuffee, | Long Island, do | do |
| Isaac Carrol, | New York, do | unknown. |
| Ezekiel Church, | Phil., Penn., | do |
| Peter Dowling, | Lewisburg, Vir., | Gov. Tomkins. |
| Wm. Denning, | New Bedford, | man-of-war. |
| Isaac Darlton, | Boston, Mass., | do |
| Thomas Denison, | Portsmouth, N. H., | man-of-war. |
| Thomas Dunn, | New York, N. Y., | unknown. |
| John Davis, | Alexandria, Vir., | man-of-war. |
| Henry Dison, | Holmes' Hole, | unknown. |
| Silas Eaton, | Phil., Penn., | M. S. Malta. |
| Dudley French, | b. Newburyport, Mass., | unknown. |
| John Fowler, | | do |
| Elias Field, | | do |
| Nicholas Gold, | North Kingston, R. I., | do |
| Wm. Goes, | New York, N. Y., | do |
| Jeremiah Gills, | b. Baltimore, Maryland, | do |
| Isaac Griffin, | Boston, Mass., | do |
| —— Gills, | New York, N. Y., | do |

| | | |
|---|---|---|
| Samuel Harvey, | North Carolina, | Impressed. |
| James Hoyd, | New York, N. Y., | man-of-war. |
| Henry Hamong, | Phil., Penn., | brig Esel, Balt. |
| Henry Holsworth, | New York, | unknown. |
| John Hopkins, | do | do |
| Samuel Hopkins, | do | do |
| Samuel Hainsly, | b. do | do |
| Wm. Hull, | b. Balt., Maryland, | do |
| Johnson Harlem, | b. New York, | do |
| James Hall, | Wainsburg, N. Y., | do |
| Wm. Hubbard, | Providence, R. I., | do |
| Peter Henrv, | Phil., Penn., | do |
| Thos. Hazaird, | Narragansett, R. I., | do |
| John Fitz, | New Bedford, Mass., | do |
| Benjamin Holbrook, | Kennebeck, do | |
| Thomas Jackson, | b. New-York, | do |
| John Jackson, | Long-Island, | do |
| Samuel Jackson, | b. Salem, Mass., | do |
| John Jackson, | b. New-Bedford, | do |
| Wm. Johnson, | Norfolk, Vir., | do |
| Zaca James, | Snowhill, Maryland, | do |
| Francis Johnson, | Bal., do | do |
| Nathan Kezer, | Newburyport, Mass., | do |
| John Jones, | Boston, do | do |
| Isaac Lemur, | do do | Impressed. |
| Andrew Lamson, | Portsmouth, N. H., | unknown. |
| John Lunderson, | New-York, | do |

| | | |
|---|---|---|
| John Lames, | Portsmouth, N. H., | brig Hunter. |
| George Lewis, | b. unknown, | unknown. |
| George Lee, | b. Salem, Mass., | do |
| Asa Freeman, | Pittyfoog, unknown. | |
| Jeremiah Miller, | Soco, Maine, | do |
| Edward Mathews, | Phil., Penn., | man-of-war. |
| John Morris, | do do | do |
| Mr. Fairlin, | Balt., Maryland, | do |
| Benjamin Morgan, | b. unknown, | do |
| Benjamin Melvin, | b. Nantucket, Mass. | do |
| John Molden, | b. Balt., Maryland, | do |
| —— Morris, | New-York, | do |
| Edw. Moulton, | Newburyport, Mass., | do |
| Henry Moore, | New-York, | do |
| John Mackey, | Portsmouth, N. H., | do |
| John Nicklas, | New-York, N. Y., | do |
| —— Owens, | Philadelphia, Penn. | |
| Richard Porter, | Wiscasset, Mass., | Impressed. |
| Thomas Parkman, | unknown. | |
| Edward Phillips, | do | |
| Elisha Paul, | Maryland. | |
| Simon Roy, | Saybrook, Connecticut. | |
| John Ride, | Philadelphia, Penn. | |
| Thomas Roberson, | Plymouth, Mass., | man-of-war. |
| John Rough, | Alexandria, Virginia. | |
| William Riley, | Philadelphia. | |
| Henry Randolph, | ——, Massachusetts. | |

| | |
|---|---|
| Robert Real, | New-York, N. Y. |
| James Roberts, | b. Wilmington, N. C. |
| Robert Roberts, | b. New-York. |
| John Ring, | Philadelphia, Penn. |
| Nathan Robinson, | unknown. |
| Morris Russell, | Savannah, Georgia. |
| William Rich, | Warrington, Conn. |
| Isaac Somendycke, | New-York. |
| George Simsons, | b. Philadelphia. |
| David Simond, | b. Alexandria, Virg., impressed. |
| John Smith, | Norfolk, do do |
| James Stanly, | New-York. |
| William Symons, | b. Charleston, S. C. |
| William Stewart, | b. unknown. |
| John Simon, | b. do |
| William Strong, | Marblehead, Mass. |
| David Stephens, | Long-Island, N. Y. |
| William Scofield, | Turkey-Hill, Oldhadam, Conn. |
| John Thompson, | Long Island, N. Y. |
| Edward Fitley, | New-York. |
| John Vanderhoven, | New-York. |
| William Welch, | Charleston, S. C. |
| Charles Wetmore, | Norwich., Con. |
| John B. Williams, | Baltimore, Md. |
| John Wells, | New-York. |
| Charles Wright, | Alexandria, Vir. |
| Charles Wilford, | New-York. |

| Charles Williams, | unknown. | |
| William Watson, | Charleston, S. C., | man-of-war. |
| William Walker, | Pelham, N. H. | |
| Jason Wood, | Philadelphia, Penn. | |
| William Wood, | do do | |
| Ezekiel Wilson, | do do | |
| William Wolf, | Savannah, Georgia. | |
| Charles Wilson, | Providence, R. I. | |
| Robert Wilson, | Newport, do | |

---

*The following is a correct list of prisoners who entered his Majesty's service at the Depot of Stapleton, from July 1813, until May 1814, copied from the clerk's books.*

| John Abrahams, | b. New-York, | Grand Napoleon. |
| John Brown, | Charleston, S. C., | Revenge. |
| John Reinbridge, | Dutchman, Tickler, Boston. | |
| Charles Burgoin, | Charleston, S. C., | Revenge. |
| Joseph Fletcher, | Portland, Mass., | Orders in Council. |
| Henry Henrick, | | do |
| Eben. Jacobs, | Newburyport, | impressed. |
| William Howard, | Philadelphia, | Fox. |
| Stephen Henry, black man. | | |
| Robert Hackley, | New-York, | unknown. |
| Mark Mason, | Philadelphia, | Fox. |
| James Marley, | Norfolk, Virg., | impressed. |
| George Russell, | New-York, | Tom of Baltimore. |
| John Smith, | | Paul Jones. |
| Francis Surges, black man. | | |

Thomas Taylor,         Maryland,         Price of Baltimore.

Charles White,        New-York,        Meteor.

---

*The following is a list of names of persons who died at Stapleton prison, from July 1813 until June 1814.*

George Morgan,  Long-Island, N. Y., Grand Napoleon.

David Smart,     New-York,      Price of Baltimore.

John Dunn,       Philadelphia, do   do

D. Francis,       Providence, R. I.,  Hebe of Philadel.

John Mitchel,    New-York,      unknown.

Isaac Watts,     Charleston, S. C.,  do

Lambert Johnson, New-York,      do

---

*The following is a list of names of persons who died at Chatham, on board the different prison-ships, from January 1813 until June 1814; at which time all the prisoners were removed to the depot at Dartmoor.*

Feb.    28, 1814 Samuel Abbet, Andover, Mass.

Feb.    19,  do  William Allen, Newport, R. I.

Jan.    4, 1813 Joseph Andrews, Marblehead.

Jan.    7,  do  Howel Baysta, Boston, Mass.

Dec.    5, 1814 Moses Blackman, Boston, do

              James Butler, unknown.

Feb.    28, 1814 William Butler, Baltimore, Md.

March 31,  do  John Adams, New-York.

Dec.      1813. Ely Bactman, Wocester county, Mass.

              Thomas Billings, New-York.

Jan.    9, 1813 Christopher Balbadge, Salem, Mass.

May      3,  do  Edward Brown, Marblehead, do

June      5,  do  Nicholas Bunker, Scituate, do

June    11,  do  Jesse Brown, Belfast, Maine.

Nov.   23,  do  Thomas Carter, Norfolk, Vir.

May      4  do  Thomas Copland, Charleston, S. C.

April   16,  do  Isaac Clough, Marblehead, Mass.

May    25,  do  —— Christy, Baltimore, U. S. gun-boat.

March  4,  do  James Davis, Somerset.

April   27,  do  John H. Downie, Salem, Mass.

July      5,  do  James Diverause, do do

April   18,  do  Benjamin Elvell, Gloucester, Mass.

May    19,  do  William Elingwood, Marblehead, Mass.

Jan.     27,  do  William Foller, Marblehead, Mass.

Mar.    27,  do  Anthony Fundy, New-York.

April   12, 1814 William Forman, Portsmouth, New Hampshire.

May    18,  do  Amos Graindy, Marblehead, Mass.

June      6, 1813 James B. Green, Alexandria, Vir.

June    25, 1814 Thomas Hutchinson, unknown.

Dec.    27,  do  George Hubbard, do

Feb.    14,  do  William Hart, do

April   17,  do  Jacob Holt, Salem, Mass.

May    —,  do  Christopher Hubbard, Baltimore, Md.

Mar.    29,  do  Samuel Head, New-York.

Feb.      5,  do  Samuel Jones, New-York, Tyger.

May    16,  do  John Johnson, Long-Island, N. Y.

Mar.    12,  do  William Light, unknown.

Feb.    23,  do  Reuben Ludlow, New-York, Tyger.

Jan.   7, do  James Lewis, Norfolk, Vir.

Mar.   30, do  James Ludlow, Greenfield, Con.

Mar.   22, do  Ezekiel Miller, New-York.

Mar.   29, do  Samuel Miller, New-York.

April   1, do  Fisher Mansfield, New-London, Con.

     Aaron Mackley, drowned escaping.

Mar.   16, do  Captain Morgan, Salem, Mass., Enterprize.

June   10, do  James Mills, Alexandria, Vir.

Mar.   29, 1813 Samuel Nelson, New-York.

Jan.   6, 1814 Hugh Nichols, Newbern, N. C.

April   3, do  William Pousland, Marblehead, Mass.

do   20, do  Clement Pair, Portland, Maine.

do   21, do  Edward Patten, Baltimore.

May   24, do  William Potter, Beverly, Mass.

June   6, do  David Pinkham, Nantucket, do

Jan.   4, do  Jared Ray, New York.

     John Roaply, New York.

Mar.   25, do  Charles Saunders, near Alexandria, Vir.

do   19, do  Proctor Simonds, unknown.

do   24, do  Ebenezer Skinner, Nantucket, Mass.

     Henry Scott, Baltimore.

     Jonathan Sawyer, Portland, Maine.

Nov.   25, 1813 Reuben Moslaird, Nantucket, Mass., Tyger, N. Y.

Feb.   16, do  Daniel Roaps, Salem, Mass.

May   9, do  John Rotter, Md.

Apr.   24, 1814 James Smith, Marblehead, Mass.

     —— Growler, Salem, do

May    28,  do  Jonathan Trueman, Portland, Maine.

Mar.    6,  do  Edward Williams, Philadelphia.

Apr.   14,  do  James Weeks, Marblehead, Mass.

do     29, 1813 Samuel Warren, unknown.

Mar.    4,  do  Richard Winchester, Gloucester, Mass.

————— Webber, Kennebeck, Maine.

Aug.   16,  do  Francis Williams, Salem, Mass.

Mar.   26,  do  Stephen Thatson, Brookfield, do

Thirty-nine names unknown—chiefly United States Infantry.

*The following contains a list of the persons who died at Dartmoor from April 1813, until the 18th February, 1815; copied from the reports of the Doctor.*

Dec.   23, 1813 Henry Alligo, New York, U. S. brig Argus.

Oct.   24,  do  Ambrose Alamond, Carthagenia, President.

Nov.    6,  do  John Adams, Washington, S. C., Greyhound.

do     21,  do  John B. Allen, N. Y., Herald.

Dec.   25, 1814 Isaac Anderson, Portsmouth, N. H., Huzzar.

do     23,  do  Joshua Andrews, Ipswich, Mass., David Porter.

do      3,  do  John Adams, N. C., America.

do     27,  do  Alexander Anderson, N. Y., Criterion.

Jan.    7,  do  Jacob Anderson, Portsmouth, N. H.

do     26,  do  Daniel Archer, Salem, Mass., Grand Turk.

do      4, 1815 Daniel Appleton, Portsmouth, N. H., U. S. Frolic.

Feb.    5, 1815 Robert Adams, Marblehead, Mass., Herald.

do     18,  do  Peter Amos, Martha's Vineyard, Mass., Invincible Napoleon.

Nov.   14,  do  Asa Allen, Boston, Herald.

May     5, 1814 Nick Blanchard.

Nov.   20, 1813 Hezekiah Bray, Boston, India.

do      23, do  John Boatman, Baltimore, Chasseur.

do       5, 1814 Lewis Bryen, Carolina, Hawke.

do      27, do  Peter Berry, died suddenly.

do      28, do  Peter Barker, Boston, Derby.

do      28, do  Peter Bin, Petersburg, Va., Independence.

do       3, 1813 Thomas Barren, Va., United States brig Argus.

Dec.     2, do  Henry Burly, New-York.

do       5, do  John Baldwin, Boston, Fox.

do       8, do  James Barret, Pennsylvania, Bury.

do      25, 1814 Henry Burbage, Va., Greyhound.

Jan.    30, do  Charles Barker.

do      27, do  Benjamin Bale, Dover, N. H., Victory.

do      20, do  Philip Blagdell, N. H., Erie.

do      14, do  James Beck, Portsmouth, N. H., impressed.

Jan.    17, 1815 Daniel Bourge, Portsmouth, N. H., Harlequin.

Feb.    11, do  George Brown, Westchester, N. Y., impressed.

do      17, do  Charles Brown, Boston, Paul Jones.

do      17, do  Moses Bailey, Philadelphia, Scorpion.

Nov.    21, 1814 John Bablista, New-York, Herald.

Jan.    23, do  John Bryson, Va., Alicant.

Dec.    29, 1814 James Booth, New-York, Mary.

Nov.    18, do  Y. S. Bates, unknown.

July     4, do  William Clarke, Va., Frolic.

Oct.    20, 1813 William Clark, South Kingston, R. I., Star of N. Y.

Jan.    16, do  Charles Cornish, Baltimore, Md., Chesapeake.

Mar.     5, do  James Combs, Bristol, D. Maine, U. S. brig Argus.

do      20, do  John Cole, Wiscasset, impressed.

April    6,  do  Benjamin Cook, Baltimore, Md., Chesapeake.

Oct.     3,  do  Deal Carter, New-York, Zebra, N. Y.

do       7,  do  John Collins, Philadelphia, Mammoth, Baltimore.

do      16,  do  John Carney or Carson, Virginia, Flash.

do      25,  do  Simeon Chandler, Duxbury, Essex.

Nov.     8,  do  Thomas Cooper, Washington, N. C., Union.

do      11,  do  James Congdon, Cambridge, Mass., Mary.

do      26,  do  John Cole, Baltimore, Md., Adeline.

Dec.     4,  do  Richard Coffee, Long Island, N. Y., America.

Jan.    17,  do  Samuel Campeach, Carthagena, President.

do      24,  do  Simeon Clark, Weathersfield, Snapdragon.

Nov.     5, 1814 William Coleman, N. C. Hawke.

May     10,  do  William Dilton, Georgetown, Argus.

Nov.    14,  do  Silas Durham, Boston, Mass., India.

Nov.    18, 1814 Amasa Dilano, New-Bedford, India.

Jan.    10,  do  William Dimamond, R. I., brig Mary.

Oct.    25, 1814 David Dunham, unknown, Fame, Baltimore.

Jan.    26,  do  William Edgar, N. J., Hepsie.

do       6, 1815 Edward Evans, Kennebunk, brig Star, N. Y.

Feb.    25, 1814 William Ferza, Granville, Mermaid.

Jan.    27,  do  James Fulford, N. C., Snapdragon.

———           Wm. Fletcher, Marblehead, Mass., Spitfire, Boston.

Dec.    23, 1813 Henry Frelitch, Liverpool, Penn., Liverpool.

Nov.    12,  do  Jesse Field, Townsend, Maine, Siron.

do      30,  do  Joshua Fowler, Boston, impressed.

Jan.    23,  do  William Fennel, Portsmouth, N. H., Harper.

Mar.    18, 1814 Thomas Foquet, Granville, brig Argus.

May —, 1813 Reuben Glass, Duxbury, Mars, of Baltimore.

April 19, 1814 Thomas Gasgiline, Martinico, W. I., Augustine.

Oct. 22, do William Gibson, N. York, Rattlesnake.

Nov. 4, do Francis Gardner, ——, R. I., Rambler.

Dec. 3, do John Gaylor, ——, North Carolina, America.

Feb. 17, 1815 James Gedman, Partsmouth, N. H., Bunker Hill.

Jan. 29, 1815 Richard Hughs, New-York, Amiable, Philadelphia.

Mar. 5, do Simeon Harress, New-York, Magdalen.

July 3, 1814 James Henry, New-York, U. S. brig Argus.

do 8, do James Hart, do Courier of Baltimore.

Nov. 9, do Isaac Hermain, Portland, Maine, Elbridge Gerry.

do 11, do James Hetrope, Cambridge, Mass., Mary.

do 24, do William Harress, Portsmouth, N. H., Portsmouth.

Dec. 24, do Dempey Hydra, ——, North Carolina, Paul Jones.

do 4, do Silas Hardison, ——, North Carolina.

Jan. 6, 1815 Elijah Hartford, St. Thomas, U. S. infantry.

Feb. 5, do Jacob Hanley, Milford, impressed.

Dec. 29, 1814 Alexander Henderson, New-York, Criterion.

Nov. 4, do William Jones, Cambridge, Mass., Hawke.

April 30, do George Jones, ——, Connecticut, Viper of Balt.

June 25, do Lambert Johnson, Middletown, N. J., Paul Jones.

do 6, do Thomas Jackson, New-York, impressed.

Nov. 2, do Alexander Johnson, Charleston, S. C., William.

do 25, do Manuel Joseph, Oporto, impressed.

Jan. 24, do Thomas Jarvis, Marblehead, Mass., Industry.

do 8, 1815 John Johannas, Salem, Mass., President.

Feb. 1, do John Johnson, New York, born in Rhode Island, Criterion.

Nov.    11, 1814 James Ketrope, Cambridge, Mary.

Feb.    3, 1815 Uriah King, Scituate, Mass., Dominick.

Nov.    3, 1814 Jesse Lasol, Martinico, President.

Aug.    5,  do  John Lewis, R. I., True-blooded Yankee.

Jan.    1,  do  James Lestar, unknown, do

Jan.    15,  do  Charles Lamson, Balt., Md., Mars, Balt.

Sept.   30, 1814 Lewis Larkins, Durham, Mass., Rolla.

Nov.    1,  do  Placid Lorly, Washington, Hawke.

Nov.    22,  do  Anthony Lamb, Conn., Grand Turk.

Dec.    30,  do  Richard Lee, Mass., brig Argus.

Jan.    27,  do  Amos Larkins, Beverly, Mass., impressed.

Feb.    4, 1815 James Laskey, Marblehead, Mass., Enterprise.

Nov.    20, 1814 Sola, Marshall, Mass., Alexandria.

Oct.    1, 1813 Thomas Morrison, Balt., Md., Messenger.

Jan.    14, 1814 Henry Moore, New York, Marmion, N. Y.

Feb.    24,  do  John Montgomery, New Bedford, impressed.

Sept.   22,  do  Manuel Martin, New Orleans, Paul Jones, N. Y.

Oct.    27,  do  Calasso Madosa, Carthagena, President.

Oct.    25,  do  Albert Mingo, New Orleans, Weezer.

Nov.    18,  do  Rollen M'Donovan, Mass., Siro.

do      18,  do  John Macky, Balt., Md., Rattlesnake.

do      20,  do  Richard Miller, Penn., Snap Dragon.

Jan.    30,  do  Joseph Midge, unknown.

Dec.    12,  do  Ezekiel Mitchell, Portland, D. Maine, Charlotte.

Feb.    5, 1815 Jesse March, Kennebunk, do M'Donough.

Feb.    14,  do  Wm. Misten, Balt., Md., impressed.

Feb.    17,  do  John Martin, Carthagena, President.

Sol Marshall, Deer Island, Mass., Mammoth.

Jan.　22, 1815 Peter Mitchell, New York, Formidable.

Nov.　15, 1813 Benj. Newbern, New York, U. S. brig Argus.

Sept.　29, 1814 Edw'd Norton, Plymouth, Mass., U. S. ship Argus.

Feb.　24, 1815 Daniel Nash, Maryland, impressed.

Oct.　7, 1814 Josiah Pettengell, Salem, Mass., Enterprise.

Nov.　4,　do　Joel Perigo, Boston, Mass., India.

March 12,　do　Samuel Pierce, Greenwich, R. I., Dart, of N. Y.

Dec.　4,　do　Samuel Peterson, Phil., Nonsuch.

Nov.　5,　do　Thomas Parker, Balt., Md., Dominique.

Nov.　26,　do　Wm. Parker, New York, Derby.

Jan.　30,　do　Charles Parker, unknown.

Nov.　3,　do　John Perkins, Pittsfield, Mass., Siro.

Nov.　7,　do　James Palmer, Portsmouth, N. H., Frolic.

do　23,　do　John Pollard, Pernambuco, S. A. Ida.

Jan.　14,　do　Aaron Peterson, Stonington, Conn., Joel Barlow.

Oct.　5,　do　John Potter, Phil., Penn., impressed.

Sept.　25,　do　Ephraim Pinkham, Wiscasset, Maine, Mammoth.

May,　1813 Horace Risley, Long-Island, N. Y., Star of N. Y.

Nov.　16, 1814 Benjamin Rinevon, Guadaloupe, West Indies, Fox.

do　12,　do　Luke Rodgers, ——, North Carolina, Fairy.

do　14,　do　David Reed, Townsend, District of Maine, America.

Dec.　29,　do　James Rooth, Norwich, Conn., Mary.

Jan.　9,　do　Silas Hardison, ——, North Carolina, Hawke.

do　22,　do　Thomas Rix, Suffolk, Vir., Labrador.

Feb.　7, 1815 Francis Roberts, St. Sebastian, Spain, Chesapeake.

Feb.　14, 1815 John Risdon, Baltimore, Pike.

do      15,  do  Samuel Robenson, Boston, Ducanavia.

Dec.     9, 1814 Samuel Robenson, Phil., Nonsuch.

Jan.    16,  do  William Saunders, Kennebunk, Maine, Mars of Baltimore.

Oct.    17,  do  William Shans, U. S. brig Argus.

do      20,  do  Francis Saul, Wiscasset, Maine, Mercury.

do      25,  do  Jacob Sawyer, Providence, R. I., impressed.

Nov.     3,  do  Richard Sperdy, ——, Virginia, Amelia.

do      20,  do  Isaac Simerson, New York, Invincible.

do      21,  do  Lewis Stow, Middletown, Conn., Tickler.

Dec.     7,  do  Jacob C. Secusa, New York, Volunteer.

do       8,  do  Nicholas Smith, Richmond, Virginia, Herald.

do      15,  do  John Stiles, Baltimore, Md., William Bayard.

Jan.    24,  do  Henry Schelding, unknown.

do      14,  do  Smith Schelding, New York, Fort Erie.

do       5, 1815 John Stow, Harlequin.

do      20,  do  John Straul, Portland, Maine, Siro.

March 15, 1814 William Sternis, Norwich, Conn., Viper of Balt.

Dec.     5,  do  William Smart, ——, Virginia, Gothland.

Jan.    28, 1815 Daniel Simons, Marblehead, Mass., Enterprise.

do      12,  do  Ebenezer Simons, unknown.

Feb.     7,  do  John Seapach, Portland, Maine, Alicant.

March  9, 1814 Eleazer Tobie, New York, True-blooded Yankee.

Feb.    25,  do  William Tyre, Springfield, Viper of Baltimore.

March 18,  do  Thomas Tagatt, Granville, Argus.

July    23,  do  Abraham Thomas, ——, Conn., P. Jones.

Sept.   26,  do  Matthew Tineman, New York, Tom Thumb.

Oct.    25,  do  John Thomas, New York, Elbridge Gerry.

Nov.    3, do  Abraham Tompkins, New York, Governor Shelby.

do     24, do  Francis Tuttle, Pernell, Maine, Leo.

Dec.    2, do  John B. Taylor, New York, Fair American.

Jan.    27, do  James Fulford, ——, North Carolina, Snap-Dragon.

Feb.    12, 1815 Samuel Tophown, Montgomery, soldier of the U. S. A.

Jan.    8, do  James Vassa, unknown, Growler.

Jan.    19, do  Daniel Very, Salem, Mass., Frolic.

Aug.    31, 1814 Nathaniel Vaughrs, Newport, R. I., Ducanavia.

Mar.    20, do  Thomas Williams, ——, Connecticut, Viper of Baltimore.

Oct.    27, do  William Williams, Georgetown, Maria, Theresa.

Dec.    5, do  William Wescott, ——, Virginia, Gothland.

Jan.    14, do  James Williams, Weathersfield, Conn., Caroline.

do     17, do  Seth Williams, Portsmouth, N. H., Harlequin.

Jan.    28, 1815 George Overt, ——, N. H., impressed.

do     8, do  Joseph Wedger, Marblehead, Mass., Growler.

Feb,    1, 1815 Joseph Williams, Gay-Head, Enterprise.

Jan.    24, 1814 Thomas Zervice, Marblehead, Mass., Industry.

do     21, do  William Young, North Carolina, Levant.

————

*The following is a list of persons who escaped from Dartmoor prison from September, 1814, the first escape, until March 13, 1815.*

Sept    20, 1814 Shapley Smith, Baltimore, Leo.

do     20, do  Henry Cottrill, Narraganset, R. I., unknown.

Oct        1814 Capt. Swain, New Bedford, Mass.

          1814 Gascoigne, unknown.

Nov        do  Henry Allen, Salem, Mass., Polly.

          John Windham, unknown.

Dec        1814—— Russell, New Bedford, Mass.

do         do  —— Howard, unknown.

Sept       do  Benjamin Prince, Portland, Maine, Magdalen.

Jan        1815 Rodgers, New York, True-blooded Yankee.

do         do  Caleb Holmes, do, unknown.

Feb        do  Joseph Langford, Baltimore, True-blooded Yankee.

Feb      6, do  George Denison, Portland, Maine, Siro of Balt.

         12, do  John W. Fletcher, Alexandria, Vir., Rattlesnake.

March 12,  do  David Flood, Portland, Maine, Impressed.

do         do  Isaiah Bunker, Philadelphia, True-blooded Yankee.

do       18, do  William Webster, unknown.

Escaped from the last date until April, six men, names unknown.

*The following is a correct list of names of prisoners who died at Dartmoor prison, from February 18, 1815, until April 20, 1815.*

Mar.     4, 1815 Archibald Allen, ——, New Jersey, impressed.

do       15,  do  William Adams, ——, Connecticut, impressed.

                 Capt. Allen, of the United States brig Argus, of wounds.

Feb      22,  do  John Butler, ——, Delaware, Semiramus.

Mar.     13,  do  Peter Burch, Philadelphia, Prosperity.

do       29,  do  Wm. Brady, Baltimore, Flash, N. Y.

do       22,  do  Henry Campbell, Philadelphia, Penn., Columbia.

April    5,  do  James Campbell, New York, impressed.

March 11,  do  Jonathan Dyer, Portsmouth, N. H., True-blooded Yankee.

Feb      25, 1815 Jon. Davis, Middle-river, Mass., ship Yorktown.

Mar.     30,  do  Benjamin Delano, Ducksbury.

Apr.     12,  do  John Devinas, ——, Ohio.

Mar.     14,  do  William Evin, ——, Rhode Island, brig Star.

Mar.   18,  do   Archibald Fogerty, ——, Massachusetts, Horatio.

Apr.   16,  do   John Francis, Norfolk, Vir., impressed.

Mar.    4,  do   Jeremiah Gardner, Newort, R. I., impressed.

Feb.   23,  do   Josiah Gun, Salem, Mass.

Mar.   24,  do   Thomas Groves, Boston, Mass., Port Mahon.

Mar.   14, 1815. Jonathan Gladding, Bristol, R. I., Rattlesnake.

Feb.   24,  do   Francis Hobden, Gloucester, Vir.

Mar.   10,  do   Abijah Holbrook, Weymouth, Derby.

Mar.   14,  do   John Hobson, Bedford, N. C., Snapdragon.

Mar.   20,  do   Joseph Haycock, Portland, Maine.

Apr.    6,  do   Henry Holden, Boston, Sultan.

Apr.    6,  do   John Haywood, ——, Vir., impressed.

Apr.   18,  do   Thomas Hall, ——, Surprise.

Feb.   22,  do   John Jennings, Gay Head, M. V. Hawke.

Feb.   23,  do   James Jones, ——, Md., impressed.

Feb.   26,  do   Peter Joseph, West Indies, President.

Feb.   24,  do   Edw. Jenkins, Cambridge, Mass., Tom of Balt.

Mar.   10,  do   Wm. Johnson, Salem, Mas. impressed.

Mar.   14,  do   John Jackson, Baltimore, do

Apr.    6,  do   Thomas Jackson, New-York, Orbit.

Apr.    6,  do   Joseph Johnson, ——, Connecticut, Paul Jones.

Feb.   26,  do   James Knapps, Baltimore, impressed.

                 John Kelly, Marblehead, Mass. Alfred.

Apr.   16,  do   Jacob Kemble, Jenet.

Apr    6,  do   William Leverett, New-York, Saratoga.

Mar.   10,  do   Capt. Lepiate, ——, N. Y. Paul Jones.

Feb.   21,  do   Edward Miller, Newark, N. J. Mammoth.

Feb.  21,  do  Charles Moutle, Stonington, Con. impressed.

Mar.  26,  do  James Morris, Baltimore, President.

Mar.  24,  do  William Mills, city of Jersey, N. J. Zebra.

Mar.  27,  do  Benjamin Marshall, ——, Massachusetts, Mindor.

Mar.  30,  do  George Moore, Boston, Mass. Chasseur.

Jan.   2,  do  John Monroe, Albany, N. Y. Rattlesnake.

Apr.   6,  do  Jabez Mann, Boston, Siro.

Mar.  10,  do  Jonathan Paul, Charleston, S. C. imp.

Mar.  15,  do  Thomas Peckham, Windham, Conn. Paul Jones.

Mar.  22,  do  Gideon Porter, ——, Rhode Island, impressed.

Apr.   1,  do  Samuel Parish, Norfolk, Vir. Grand Napoleon.

Feb.  23,  do  Joseph Quion, Salem, Mass. Herald.

Mar.   2,  do  Joseph Rasom, Wiscasset, Maine, Ned of Balt.

Mar.   2,  do  Joseph Robenson, do do do

Apr.   1,  do  James Robenson, ——, Mass. Price of Baltimore.

Apr.  18,  do  William Robenson.

Mar.  20,  do  Jeremiah Stanwood, Newburyport, Mass. imp.

Mar.  17,  do  Silas Squibs, New-London, Conn. Hope-packet.

Feb.  22,  do  Martin Sutten, New Bedford, Mass. Lion.

Mar.   4,  do  David Shute, Salem, Mass. impressed.

Mar.   5,  do  Andrew Smith, Indian River, Tom.

Mar.  14,  do  Joseph Salesbury, ——, Mass. Zenith.

Mar.  16,  do  Theodore Snell, —— Rhode Island, a soldier.

Mar.  16,  do  Stephen Stacy, Marblehead, Mass. Ohio.

Feb.  21,  do  Henry Thomas, Cambridge, Mass. Derby.

April  14, 1815  Richard Smith, Grand Turk.

Feb.  21,  do  David Turner, Boston, Derby.

April   6,  do  John Turner, ——, Mass. Rattlesnake.

April  18,  do  William Thompson, Siro.

Feb.   25,  do  Darius Villius, Providence, R. I. Frolic.

Mar.   10,  do  Charles Williams, New-London, Connecticut.

Mar.   17,  do  Samuel Williams, ——, Mass. Scorpion.

Mar.   26,  do  Edward Williams, ——, Va. impressed.

April   6,  do  John Washington, Cooperstown, Md. Rolla.

---

*Died at Ashberton during the war,*

Mar. 10, 1815 B. Elvel, Gloucester, Mass. Firefly.

Mar. 25,  do  Abraham Burnham, ——, Mass. Price.

---

## SUPPLEMENT OF SOME MATTERS OBTAINED SINCE THE PRECEDING PAGES WERE WRITTEN.

Copy of a letter from Lieut. N. D. NICHOLSON, of the late United States brig *Syren*, to Capt. SAMUEL EVANS, commanding naval officer at New-York.

NEW-YORK, August 24, 1815.

SIR:

Conceiving it my duty to make known the treatment exhibited by the British officers and men, to those who are so unfortunate as to fall into their power, I am induced to acquaint you with the following circumstances:

After the surrender of the *Syren* to the *Medway*, the officers and crew of the former were removed to the latter; the crew not being allowed the privilege of taking their clothing, &c., with them,—so that the prize-crew had a fair opportunity of plundering such articles as they thought proper; which opportunity they took care to profit by, as many of our men were pillaged of all they possessed, excepting what they had on at the time; and the officers in like manner were plundered on board the *Medway*. The midshipmen, some of them, were completely stripped; others lost their watches, &c. For my own part, I came off with the loss of about half my clothing, and thought myself well off when compared with the losses of my shipmates.

The morning after our capture, we were mustered on the quarter-deck, to undergo a search; the men were then stripped to the skin, and their clothing not returned; so that many of them were left without any thing more then a shirt and trowsers. The next day, Mr. Barton (the first lieutenant of the *Medway*) distributed the clothing he had taken from our men, to his quarter-masters and quarter-gunners, in my presence.

After being on board the *Medway* five weeks, we were landed at Simon-Town, twenty-five miles to the eastward of the Cape of Good Hope; myself and brother officers paroled, and the men marched to Cape-Town under an escort of dragoons; being obliged to ford a lake on the march, where the boys were compelled to go over on the backs of the tall men; this march of twenty-five miles was performed in one day, and without shoes or food; the latter article they were kept without four and twenty hours; their shoes were stolen by the crew of the *Medway* while they were asleep. After remaining in this situation nearly eight months, without bed or bedding, (they were not even furnished with straw, and their hammocks were taken on a plea of their being public property,) we were all embarked in different men-of-war and Indiamen for England; myself, and about sixty officers and men, in the Cumberland, seventy-four, Captain Baker, were all put on the lower gun-deck without distinction, among their own crew, and fed on prisoners' allowance; and on my remonstrating with the captain for receiving such treatment, he ordered me off the quarter-deck, with a threat, at the same time, to put me in irons.

We remained in this situation eighteen days, after which Lieut. German, Gordon, and myself, were removed to the Grampus, thirty, at St. Helena, admitted to the ward-room mess, and treated with civility.

With respect, I have the honor,
&c.,

N. D. NICHOLSON.

CAPT. SAMUEL EVANS.

---

**FOOTNOTES:**

[1] This man belonged to Portsmouth, N. H.

Milton Keynes UK
Ingram Content Group UK Ltd.
UKHW030625061024
449204UK00004B/322